IMMEMORIAL

LAUREN MARKHAM

TRANSIT
BOOKS

Published by Transit Books
1250 Addison St #103, Berkeley, CA 94702
www.transitbooks.org

ISBN: 979-8-893389-03-6 (paperback)
Cover design by Anna Morrison | Typesetting by Transit Books
Printed in the United States of America

9 8 7 6 5 4 3 2 1

This project is supported in part by a grant from the National
Endowment for the Arts.

for Clio

1.

Years ago, before I became a parent, I had a low-paid job that required me to travel to Slovenia every summer and drive a bunch of writing students around the country in a large, unwieldy van. My employers treated me poorly, but back then you could ask me to do anything if it involved a free plane ticket. The world was big and it beckoned; I thought only of what I could afford and little of its environmental costs.

My flight home from Slovenia almost always passed over Greenland. For the better part of an hour, I would press my face against the window to become transfixed by the great, frozen world below. I knew to sit on the right side of the plane and stay awake long enough to catch sight of it—all that precious ice. Once it came into view I'd feel newly shaken by its beauty, as if encountering it for the first time, though the sight would also awaken all the memories of years past when I'd stared out a window just like this one with the same unplaceable longing for the mysterious, unknown-to-me landscape down below. Memory often functions this way: in layers, as echo. Much of this ice would be gone soon, I knew. This annual, sky-high ritual became an anticipatory memorial to that vanishing world.

The circumstances of my life changed and I stopped going to Slovenia every summer. I mostly traveled as a journalist now—more free plane tickets. Meanwhile, the climate crisis was becoming harder to ignore. It was something I wrote a lot about in the magazines that paid me to travel the world. (The irony was not lost on me.) A couple years ago, when I was returning from a reporting trip in Greece, my plane passed over the Alps. The snow-mantled crags reminded me of Greenland, of the way it felt to behold an astonishing landscape from above with an awareness that it was slipping away. By then, air travel had become a more fraught enterprise. In 2017, *complicit* was named a word of the year, but ever since, it had paradoxically become something of a linguistic escape hatch: simply admit your complicity and then you'd subverted it, free now to fly on by to the next destination, to the rest of your complicit life. When it came to the ice I was complicit, I was in awe, I was stuck in that awe and in that complicity and in my seat on that Boeing 777.

I longed for that alpine ice like one longs for a dead thing, but the ice was right there. Was it that I longed to be down upon the ice, enjoying its final days? Or was I simply longing for its fixedness upon the map of the world? Any attempt to parse the exact contours of this desire or to put it into words melted like a handful of snow. So I placed my phone against the window and took pictures of the Alps' jagged winter shadows, as if trying to secure the scene in place.

"The snow-dusted Alps," I posted on Instagram from my layover in Switzerland. "What's a word for the simultaneous enchantment of beholding this breathtaking world from above, and the feeling of complicity in its destruction?"

"Guiltchantment?" my friend Holly replied.

"*Blissonance* is our most popular term for this very

real phenomena ♥," posted someone from an account called @thebureauoflinguisticalreality.

The Bureau of Linguistical Reality—it sounded both ominous and spellbinding, like a trapdoor situated deep in the forest. How could one help but fall through? I looked them up. The operation was the brainchild of Bay Area artists Alicia Escott and Heidi Quante, who, like me, had found themselves "at a loss for words to describe the very real emotions and feelings" of a rapidly changing world. Escott is Cofounder and Executive Director of Interspecies Advancement and Treasurer of Geologic Time; Quante is Cofounder and Chief Catalyst of New Words and Worlds. The artists graft their work to the concept of "linguistic relativity," which suggests that the language available to its speakers determines how they see the world and thus how they act within it.

"We reference this term playfully," the founders write, "but believe sincerely that until we have the language to describe the changing world around us, we will not be able to fully grasp what is happening."

The Bureau publishes their ever-expanding dictionary online, and I scrolled through their words, entranced by the possibilities of a shape-shifting language to match the shape-shifting world.

Gwilt: "To cause wilting in plants by not providing proper horticultural care out of concern for water consumption, especially during a time of drought. The feeling of regret and responsibility for their wilting."

Marsification: "The drive to turn relatively lifeless Mars into a new Earth while effectively turning biodiverse Earth into Mars . . . The expansion of colonial fantasy beyond the atmosphere of the Earth. 'Manifest Destiny to the stars.'"

Pre-Traumatic Stress Disorder: "A condition in which a researcher experiences symptoms of trauma as they learn more about the future as it pertains to climate change and watch the world around them not making necessary precautions."

At the time I'd been reading a fair bit about climate-related trauma. As the activist Britt Wray writes in her book *Generation Dread*, "Climate change and ecological breakdown—ongoing threats to life that they are—create their own order of trauma and become a new lens through which we see the world."

I'd also been thinking a lot about memory, and forgetting, and how those unsteady acts of the mind map to grief. The feeling of grieving something that isn't yet gone, and whose disappearance isn't fully certain, nor can its timeline be predicted, is an eerie, off-putting one. How do we mourn the abstracted casualties of the future? Grief can feel like a physical mass. Where to put it?

This brought me back to language, the importance of effectively naming and ordering things. In her book, Wray suggests that we must "find a container for our overwhelming emotions." I pictured a rummage-sale heap of baskets and tea tins and old cigar boxes, each perfectly suited to hold what was placed inside. I had shared the photograph on Instagram because I had an instinct that acknowledging my complicity would somehow make me feel better about it, but also because I was searching for company in my grief and a place for it to go. Surely there was a better container than an iPhone photograph, an online post. Where do we go to mourn? We go to gravesites and to holy places. And we go to memorials.

Memorials had been something of a lifelong fascination for me. If grief is the cavernous emotion nearly ubiquitous to human life, and mourning is the ritualized enactment of that feeling, then a memorial seemed to offer a space for both the feeling and its enactment to be made communally manifest in the

LAUREN MARKHAM • 13

physical world. Were there memorials to hold our climate grief? Maybe this was what I'd been longing for up above those iced-over worlds.

But here was another problem of language, because what I wanted wasn't a memorial, exactly. Memorials are about time, as Paisley Rekdal has written. "The conflicts of the present," she argues in the *Kenyon Review*, "must be framed by an understanding of our past and an awareness of the conflict's future ramifications; in that, memorials must have a relationship with the passage of time." What I sought from such a memorial was not just an understanding of the past as it related to the contemporary climate emergency and its future ramifications. I wanted a space to remember and mourn the vanishing future itself: a syntactical problem, for starters, and one that required time to be bent like a boomerang.

And anyway, I wanted to both conjure these memorial spaces and also better understand my longing for them. What need was my yearning trying to sate? And what did such yearning suggest about grief and memory in the age of climate emergency, about the future of memory in our landscape of cataclysmic planetary loss? The yearning itself felt like a bucket with a hole in it—I was all tangled up now. Was there a word for this desire to memorialize what I'd come to think of as "the future gone"? I needed help from the Bureau of Linguistical Reality.

So I sent them an email. "I am in need of a word," I wrote, "and perhaps you two are just the people to help." I hastily described what I was after: a word that expresses "the desire to memorialize something that is in the process of being lost—a landscape, for instance, or a species, or a birdsong—to erect a memory temple, or shrine, or lyric monument of sorts, to the feeling of losing something as it is going." I struggled with the words to describe the word I wanted.

I got a quick reply. "Would love to collaborate with you to create a neologism for the memorializing phenomena below." We arranged a time to talk.

2.

In 1980, a Yale undergraduate enrolled in a seminar on funereal architecture. The Vietnam Veteran's Memorial Fund had sent out a call for proposals for the construction of a new memorial, to be erected on the Washington Mall. As an academic exercise, the students in the Yale class were assigned the task of coming up with a proposal for the memorial's design.

Maya Lin was only twenty-one years old when she enrolled in the class at Yale, but she had been studying memorials for years. She would later write of her disappointment in the majority of the designs she'd been presented with at university. Most memorials, she found, were largely exercises in nationalism that commemorated the past with some degree of emptiness. These structures, she wrote, "carried larger, more general messages about a leader's victory or accomplishments rather than the lives lost."

Lin used her school assignments to advance a different kind of design, but her efforts were generally met with contempt. Early in her college career, a professor asked his students to design a memorial for those who died in World War II. Lin submitted her assignment, which she described as "a tomb-like underground structure that I deliberately made to be a very futile and frustrating experience," one that mirrored what she imagined to be the experience of fighting in a war. In response, Lin's professor roundly chastised her. If he were a family member of someone who'd died in the war, he snipped, he would be horrified to visit her memorial.

But this didn't sway her vision. When it came to developing a design for the Vietnam Memorial assignment, Lin was not interested in merely lionizing the dead, but building a space where the living could mourn.

"I wanted to create a memorial that everyone would be able to respond to, regardless of whether one thought our country should or should not have participated in the war," she wrote.

She was troubled by the fact that most memorials failed to acknowledge individuals, merely lumping the dead into a monolith. This was particularly true in the many World War I memorials she'd studied. There was an exception, though—a memorial to those that died in World War I's Battle of the Somme that named every single known member of the dead. It was from this memorial that she got the idea to include a comprehensive list of dead soldiers in her Vietnam Memorial assignment.

But what form would the memorial take? The truth was that Lin had no interest in figurative designs. As tributes, she felt, they limited the imagination; they seemed to instruct visitors in how to remember and mourn. What she wanted to create was both a physical and psychic space for feeling. Lin traveled to the site in order to conjure it. When she arrived at the mall, she later described how she was struck by the space's beauty and tranquility. "I had a simple impulse to cut into the earth," she wrote.

I imagined taking a knife and cutting into the earth, opening it up, an initial violence and pain that in time would heal. The grass would grow back, but the initial cut would remain a pure flat surface in the earth with a polished, mirrored surface, much like the surface on a geode when you cut it and polish the edge . . . It would be an interface, between our world and the quieter, darker, more peaceful world beyond . . . I never looked at the memorial as a wall, an object, but as an edge to the earth, an opened side.

Lin submitted her design to both her professor and the selection committee. Her professor gave her a B. But of the more than 1,400 designs submitted for official review (including a design submitted by her professor), the committee chose Lin's: a sleek, unabashedly modern design that trafficked primarily in metaphor.

Much of the general public was outraged at this choice. First and foremost, the memorial was conceived by a young woman—a young woman of color, at that—with little architectural experience. But her critics were most horrified at what they saw as the reductive nature of the design. Until now, the vast majority of war memorials were obvious statuaries: figurative tributes to leaders or to the heroic fallen or to victory itself. Lin's design was merely shapes and names situated against the skyline. Where was the narrative, the iconography of battle and sacrifice for country?

★★★

What people wanted is now more commonly termed a monument: a representational statue, as Erika Doss puts it in her book *Memorial Mania*, to "commemorate great men and moments." Doss points out that the term memorial and monument are now used almost interchangeably in the U.S. cultural vernacular, even though the moniker of memorial is a more common designation, and one that carries "greater cachet." This is perhaps because we have entered an era of toppling valorous, absolutist versions of history—an era of toppling monuments themselves. What we now tend to call memorials, the scholar Wilbur Zelinsky says, are more "multivalent" in nature than, say, a statue of a man once or still thought great by a certain group of people.

In the past century, many a writer and critic have gone so far as to declare the death of the monument. "The very notion of a modern monument is a contradiction in terms," wrote the historian Lewis Mumford in 1937. "If it is a monument, it cannot be modern, and if it is modern, it cannot be a monument." The atrocities of World War II only seemed to strengthen this notion. "No! No victory arches! It's all too terrible a disaster to make into a public emblem," Doss quotes a journalist writing in 1943.

Doss contends that in the wake of the war, U.S. commemorative practices largely shifted "from 'official' national narratives to the subjective symbolic expressions of multiple American publics." Modernism's proclivities were at play here too: the mandate to break convention and to deviate from figuration, as well as the emerging cultural preoccupation with "irony, ambivalence, interruption, and self-criticality." In Doss's view, the turn of the previous century had ushered in "statue mania," a monument-building spree to address anxieties about the nation-state and national unity. Today, while such figurative monuments may have gone out of style, Doss argues that the desire to commemorate never died. Seemingly everyone has a grief-stricken cause to remember. Now that "demands for the symbolic expression of particular concerns have never been stronger," statue mania has been replaced by memorial mania, driven by our national grappling with the politics of representation and memory—questions of how our history is narrated, how to reckon with past wrongs, and how to understand who, fundamentally, we are as a people. These "memory aids," as Doss calls them, "are materialist modes of privileging particular histories and values."

As Viet Thanh Nguyen has famously written, "All wars are fought twice, the first time on the battlefield, the second time in memory." What's most interesting to him about memorials is not so much the thing that gets built, but the argument over what to build and how to build it. Memorials are a battleground of truth, since the memorial builder, along with the forces that propel and bolster her, is at her core a memory maker.

★★★

Thousands of veterans protested Lin's memorial before she'd even broken ground, seeing this design as a continuation of the lethal and longtime trend of sidelining the costs of the Vietnam War on its veterans. *The Washington Post* proclaimed it "an Asian memorial for an Asian war." Politician Ross Perot suggested that, instead of such a memorial, the veterans should get something more uplifting, like a parade. "To bury them now in a black stone sarcophagus," one critic wrote, "sunk into a hollow in the earth below eye level, is like spitting on their graves."

Even the design's supporters tried to disrupt Lin's vision in order to forge compromise or impose their own ideas. Instead of the names appearing in chronological order of death, the sponsoring architecture firm wanted to put them in alphabetical order—which, Lin wrote, "would break the strength of the timeline, interrupting the real-time experience of the piece." People also wanted her to add historical text about the war itself, but she was adamant that the memorial be entirely focused on the memory of the dead.

This process required Lin to conceal her own views about the war. "Throughout this time I was very careful not to discuss my political beliefs; I played it extremely naive about politics, instead turning the issue into a strictly aesthetic one."

Meanwhile, the detractors proposed changing the color of the stone from black to white—more in line with the neoclassical monument style—and adding a figurative statue of soldiers on top or in front of the wall. Lin likened this to painting a mustache upon someone else's portrait. She stayed steadfast to her vision, and eventually, thanks to the support of many thousands of donors and some celebrity boosters, her memorial was built. (By way of compromise, a lifelike statue of three soldiers was built in a remote corner of the site.)

In spite of all the controversy, once Lin's memorial was built, its ability to move people was astonishing. The text was so small—"less than half an inch, which is unheard of in monument type sizing"—that visitors were forced to approach the wall in order to read it, creating a feeling of raw intimacy within the grandness of the scale. That close to the wall, a visitor couldn't help but see their own reflection cast upon the names of the dead, and thus be confronted with their own aliveness, and even, perhaps, complicity. Many of the veterans who had once vehemently protested the memorial were deeply affected.

"Until the memorial was built," Lin reflected, "I don't think they realized that the design was experiential and cathartic, and, most importantly, designed not for me, but for them."

In other words, abstraction worked. "No one could any longer argue that pure form was incapable of expressing profound emotion," wrote Adam Gopnik in *The New Yorker* years later. "The laconic eloquence of the minimal gesture, its potent lack of insincere rhetoric and overstatement, was apparent." The memorial really moved people.

All around the globe, Lin is now widely seen as the torchbearer of this new, more interpretive form of memorial structure. Memorials in this lineage tend to traffic in metaphor and a spirit of cocreation between the visitor, the space's creator, what or who is being remembered, the grief associated with that memory, and the space itself. "My work," says the British artist Rachel Whiteread of her Vienna Holocaust Memorial, seeks to "mummify the air in the room."

The impulse to build a memorial is born of this desire to determine the quality of the air in the room, its emotional tenor. "Because memories are abstract," writes journalist Spencer Bailey in *In Memory Of*, "so too must memorials be."

3.

"A small war had ended," begins Mary Ruefle's poem "Monument." "Like all wars, it was terrible. Things which had stood in existence were now vanished. I had come back because I had survived and survivors come back, there is nothing else left for them to do."

The speaker describes the stunned sensation of walking around the capital's park, watching ducks on a warm day, "which was not the heat of war, which had engulfed them, but the warmth of expansion, in which would grow the idea of a memorial to the war, which had ended, and of which I was a veteran architect. I knew I would be called upon for my ideas in regards to this memorial and I had entered the park aimlessly, trying to escape my ideas." (Note here the blurred lines between monument, as the poem is titled, and memorial, which is what the speaker will be charged to design.)

The speaker both resists the idea of a memorial— for how to summarize or encapsulate the momentousness of such "conflagration"?—and imagines absurdist designs for it. After picturing a favorite dessert of cherries jubilee, the speaker "had in [her] mind the idea of submitting to the committee a drawing of an enormous plate of cherries, perpetually burning, to be set in the center of the park, as a memorial to the war, that acre of conflagration."

Like in Ruefle's poem, most memorials are made to remember the victims of human-made atrocities —war, genocide, mass shootings, terrorist attacks. But in the age of rapid climate change, when every corner of the planet risks becoming its own "acre of conflagration," the sort of memorial I craved was far more amorphous and vast in terms of both the victims it memorialized and its purpose. A plate of cherries, forever burning: perhaps, if it weren't for the substantial dose of carbon it would emit, an excellent proposal.

One of the functions of a memorial is to offer a space for communal mourning and remembrance. Even if a person's memorial-induced catharsis takes place privately, it does so side by side with others. Such experiential companionship was another reason the memorial format was alluring to me. I know I'm not alone in my climate grief—or eco-grief, or eco-anxiety, as it's otherwise known. According to a recent Yale study, roughly 7 percent of U.S. adults are experiencing some form of climate anxiety (a search term that increased over 500 percent between 2020 and 2021.) Youth are hit worst of all. In a 2021 survey of ten different countries, 60 percent of youth reported feeling very or extremely worried about the future of the planet. This worry, many said, affected their ability to function in their daily lives, the choices they made, the closeness and quality of their relationships, their general health, and what they felt was possible for their futures.

Part of the trouble with metabolizing climate grief is that to do so requires grieving many abstractions at once. A person grieves the species and landscapes and people—both dear and unknown to them—that the Anthropocene has fundamentally altered or destroyed. There's also the painful truth to grieve that humans are the ones to blame, and the powerlessness one may feel in the face of the machinery causing climate catastrophe is also freighted with grief. And then there is that particularly unsteady, ghostly form of anticipatory grief for losses that are at once certain—we know the glaciers will melt and the sea will rise and the forests will burn—and not yet fully known in terms of their timeline or precise manifestation. The nature and scope of future devastation is contingent upon what action is taken, which brings a person back to the confounding, grief-stricken collision course between one's sense of personal responsibility for the future and powerlessness over it.

It takes some coming to terms with the simultaneous truths that we are small amid the mighty forces of destruction and also capable of effecting change, that things are dire but not all hope is lost, that we are living through apocalypse and a time of great possibility all at once. It can be dizzying to hold all these things—and the grief itself can get in the way.

It's also disorienting to move through a transfiguring world. Not long ago, when I was six months pregnant, my partner and I flew to southern Mexico to spend some time at the beach. We stayed a few miles up the coast from a steady surf break with a lip you could ride all the way to shore. Our rental was paradise in the most prototypical, postcard sense of the word: silhouettes of gently bending palm trees, a view of the ocean and its blush-colored sunsets, a thatched roof, our open-air bedroom allowing the sound of the sea's effervescent churn to cradle us through the night. The first morning, Ben left before daybreak to greet the waves. I got up a few hours later, meeting a sky so broad and bright that it was as if someone had flung the shutters open upon the entire universe, letting in all its light. I headed to the beach. It was indeed beautiful, but I noted something strange about the water. The sand was covered with a rust-colored foam. I scurried uphill with each wave to avoid the frothy heaps.

And then I almost stepped on a dead puffer fish lying on the sand. It was bloated, its skin distended like a spiked, too-tight balloon. Because its eyes were popped wide open, the creature gave the appearance of looking both shocked and ready to explode.

I was so taken with this one dead fish that it took me a while to notice another one just a few feet away, and then another, and another. I scanned the beach. There were hundreds of these aquatic corpses scattered upon the sand far into the distance, as though someone had detonated a bomb in the shallows. It wasn't just puffer fish, but also torpedo-shaped creatures the length of my forearm with snouts like bayonets, gleaming silver flounders, a speckled fellow smaller than my palm whose lips were fixed in a cartoonish pucker.

The waves tossed the puffer fish, and I avoided the cadavers as though they were both precious objects I might break and deadly land mines. But even so I nearly walked across a four-foot nurse shark, curled sagging and dead upon the sand.

Like I had above Greenland and the Alps, I took out my phone. It was pure instinct. I snapped picture after picture, unable to stop myself from adjusting the dead fish within the frames, leaning and bending for the right angle, settling down onto my knees. There was something sacrilegious about it, and I was aware of the screen's utility in both connecting me to and distancing me from death: the particular deaths before me, and whatever deadly force had scattered them onto the beach.

A red tide, it turned out, had recently swept the coast of Guerrero. Climate change causes a warming sea in which toxic algae can bloom suddenly and far more frequently, suffocating the creatures that make that sea their home.

It would be months before I looked at the pictures of the dead fish. But I didn't delete them. They were stored alongside so many other ghosts: photos I'd taken of the fire-charred hillsides of the Sierra not far from where I live, the piles of plastic fishermen pulled into their nets from the Aegean in Greece, the destroyed barn I once saw in Vermont after Hurricane Irene, sliced from its home along the riverbanks and deposited hundreds of yards downstream as if a severed body, nerve ends still wriggling.

I had long feared that my instinctual desire to record the ravages of climate change was a ghoulish effort to *capture*, in the rough language of social media, and to use what I caught to perform feelings for others—not merely as an act of showmanship, but out of a failure to sort out how to adequately feel and what to do about it.

But now I was beginning to suspect that this instinct was something more complex: an almost biological impulse to record what was becoming invisible, not all that distinct from my impulse toward memorial. Writing of climate trauma in *Generation Dread*, Wray speaks of a generational "capture" imperative in a sense distinct from the empty social media blip. "Dread is a resource floating freely in the air," she writes, "and it's this generation's job to capture it." She argues that, if properly harnessed, such dread can be a generative force that "[brings] about justice-oriented societal shifts." She's speaking of a kind of alchemy—turning grief into something of value for ourselves and for the world.

It seemed to me my photographs were, in part, a gesture toward action—something to *do* rather than just something to feel. Could grief be a raw material of creation? Could memories of the vanishing world be not merely vessels for grief, but an alchemical force to transform that grief into something else?

Writing had always been that vessel. But the container wasn't working like it used to, as if its latch had broken or its bottom panel had warped and cracked. Sentences had once come easily, but now I grasped for the right words. There didn't seem to be enough of them. When I turned in a draft about imperiled forests to an editor, he pointed out that I'd used the word *vast* fifteen different times.

The root problem seemed to be a matter of faith. On my most doleful days, I questioned what words could accomplish, and, if anything, whether it would be nearly fast enough. What good were words when the world was burning? These questions had always been lurking in the corner, but now they crouched upon my shoulders each time I sat down at my desk. It was beginning to feel like anything I wrote about climate change or other urgent social matters was either a feeble finger wag or merely a double underline: a reminder of things everyone already knew.

It was destabilizing to have my medium turn against me, or me, it. And it wasn't just the act of writing—it was also words themselves. What did it mean that my ordering principles no longer functioned as such—that the places I went (words, books) to most deeply feel were vanishing in substance, like the fish? Semantic satiation is the term for that unnerving occurrence when a word, having been looked at or considered for too long, ceases to hold any meaning—becoming, essentially, gobbledygook, mush. Sea, sea, sea, sea. Puffer fish, puffer fish. Future, future, future, future. Words were not only losing their power, but also their meaning. They were disintegrating all around me, item by item and feeling by feeling, fish by fish by fish.

4.

In order to understand the art and function of memorial, we must perhaps first probe the art and function of memory. Memory, according to the sociologist Maurice Halbwachs, is a collective enterprise—a retrospective impression of the many, not just the one. Rather than recalling the event as it actually happened, we instead tend to remember the *memory* of the event, which we have filed away in a sort of catalog. As real as they may feel to us, our personal memories aren't faithful reconstructions of the past, but rather mediated renovations formed by a host of external forces, including stories we've been told, conversations we've had, museums we've visited, history texts we've read, and political rhetoric that has seeped into our feed. (This is all true, too, of the high art and artifice of memory: memorial.)

"No memory is possible," he wrote, "outside frameworks used by people living in society to determine and retrieve their recollections." Memory is not only susceptible to outside influence—how someone else instructs us to understand a past event, how an event is described in the larger body politic—but it can also fall prey to tampering. Memory is thus often wielded for power.

"Society from time to time obligates people not just to reproduce in thought previous events of their lives," Halbwachs writes, "but also to touch them up, to shorten them, or to complete them." The memory process is rather like an endless game of telephone, or a photocopy of a photocopy of a photocopy, the image more off-kilter and pocked with debris with each passing run.

Another way of thinking about memory is that it is ever forming itself, a constantly mutating commodity. As psychologist and researcher Martin Seligman writes, "The brain's long-term memory has often been compared to an archive, but that's not its primary purpose. Instead of faithfully recording the past, it keeps rewriting history."

Much as we may understand in the big picture that memory is a fallible, tricky business, most of us still hold our own memories as fact. Suggesting otherwise can constitute a personal threat, for memories are the building blocks of a person's reality. It's unsettling to have this reality upended. Calling someone's personal memory into question is destabilizing enough; questioning *collective* memory can feel to that collective like an act of erasure or even of aggression.

The collective is the genesis, the guardian, and the arbiter of memory. Memories, as Halbwachs argues, "are part of a totality of thoughts common to a group." If many people believe a certain thing to have happened or imbue a past event with a certain meaning, then it is much harder to prove—or even suggest—that this reality is wrong. This is due, in part, to what Viet Thanh Nguyen refers to as the "industries of memory," which are comprised of "the material and ideological forces that determine how and why memories are produced and circulated."

As his term suggests, an industry of memory is not necessarily a benign force. Take the insistent memory-making within U.S. history as it has been, until quite recently, taught in most schools: as an exceptionalist project with the sidelined and already atoned-for exceptions of genocide and enslavement. As Clint Smith writes, "America will never be the country it wants to be until it properly remembers what it did (and does) to Black people." The more projects emerge that spotlight these central horrors of the U.S. American story (think *The 1619 Project*), and the more space they take in mainstream discourse—as counter-memory projects, one might say—the more local and state governments engage in counter-counter-memory projects: erasing facts (that Rosa Parks was asked to move to the back of the bus because she was Black) and words (*gay*, *trans*) from textbooks, for instance, even banning the teaching of race and racism in public schools. Collective memory can be both a battleground and a spoil of war.

In Smith's book *How the Word is Passed*, he visits sites where the collective memory of enslavement has been erased, sanitized, sidestepped, even celebrated.

"As I traveled across the country visiting these places," he writes, "I found lapses and distortions that would have been shocking if they weren't so depressingly familiar: a cemetery where the Confederate dead are revered as heroes; a maximum-security prison built on top of a former plantation, where prisoners were once tasked with building the deathbed upon which executions would take place; a former plantation where Black employees were once made to dress as enslaved people and give tours to white visitors." The narratives such places cement serve those nostalgic for the supremacist past, those hell-bent on forgetting its supremacist contours, and even those uncomfortable with their own connections to historical violence. Politicians routinely capitalize on the nostalgia and amnesia of such memory projects for money and for votes.

"Contemporary American memorials," writes Doss in *Memorial Mania*, "embody the feelings of particular publics at particular historical moments, and frame cultural narratives about self-identity and national purpose."

In his book, Smith investigates these enshrinements of enslavement alongside the contemporary movement to topple them: monuments to the Confederacy, for instance, to enslavers, to genocidaires and conquistadors. In this age of reexamining national stories and lionized heroes, many domineering narratives of the past are eroding as a narrative complexity and even multiplicity unfurls. It is in this spirit that so many call for old monuments to be removed and, in response, that so many others are doubling down on historic amnesia (remembering the Confederacy, for instance, as a lost Eden, bygone glory days). Politicians of the latter category work to convince voters that outsiders are trying to steal, tarnish, and bury their history. But history is just selective memory dressed up as fact. What is really at stake here is memory itself.

Public memory is bound to shift with the times, and, along with it, its artifacts. As a statement penned by the American Historical Association in the wake of the 2017 Charlottesville riot reads, a monument "is not history itself," but "commemorates an aspect of history, representing a moment in the past when a public or private decision defined who would be honored in a community's public spaces." By virtue of its pride of place in the public sphere, a monument further cements the way the past is narrated and remembered.

How do we want to remember? The American Historical Association's statement bids us to keep in mind that history is both a set of facts and their interpretations. "To remove a monument, or to change the name of a school or street, is not to erase history, but rather to alter or call attention to a previous interpretation of history." If the collective is always changing, it follows that its memory will too.

★★★

The fact that memory keeps rewriting itself, explains Seligman, isn't necessarily a bad thing. "It's a feature, not a bug," he explains. In the collective context, this rewriting is the very mechanism that allows us to reexamine the past and the way it's been remembered, allowing us to imagine a different future. In spite of the messiness of collective memory, humans tend to share a deep desire to remember together. (So do elephants, it turns out, and crows and octopi and myriad other species of animals; so, even, do some species of trees.) When a tragedy has occurred or something has been lost, we mourn via acts of memory: rituals such as burials, vigils, the building of altars, public demonstrations, national holidays. And, of course, memorials. As Rekdal suggests, memorials are about time; the function of a memorial is to write a backward story, paradoxically, toward the future.

In 2018, I traveled with students and teachers from Oakland International High School—a school serving entirely newly arrived immigrant students—to Montgomery, Alabama, to learn more about racial violence and U.S. history, and to examine how this history has been constructed and deconstructed and reconstructed over time. The first morning we walked through the streets of Montgomery to see the sites: the first White House of the Confederacy, where Jefferson Davis took up his insurrectionist throne; the site of Rosa Parks's arrest; the Dexter Avenue King Memorial Baptist Church, where Dr. King sang his sermons. Eventually, we trudged up to the Alabama State Capitol, a neoclassical building situated atop a grassy hill like a cake topper.

We came upon an eighty-eight-foot-tall rounded obelisk atop which a human figure clutches a flag in one hand and a spear in the other. One of the teachers bent down to a placard. "It's a monument to the Confederacy," she said. We'd read so much about these monuments but still found ourselves shocked to be standing in front of one, in disbelief at its size and grandeur. Intended to honor the 122,000 Alabamans who fought on behalf of the Confederacy, the monument was built in 1898, we learned, long after the Civil War had ended and the Confederacy had lost.

"They are all the hollow echoes of an expiring breath," Lewis Mumford wrote of monuments just before declaring their death.

We circled this heap of stone in various states of stupefaction.

"Why is this here?" asked a student named Lar Kpaw. He had been born in a Thai refugee camp, his parents having fled ethnic cleansing in their home in what was then Burma, and had resettled to the U.S. a few years prior. His question had no edge; it wasn't inflected with anger or blame or outrage, wasn't a rhetorical attempt to make an obvious point. He meant it earnestly. Why is this here? The debate over Confederate monuments was new to him, as was the history of the U.S. Civil War and its long shadow. Knowing what he knew, why would the state of Alabama, belonging as it did to the United States, want to honor a war fought, as he had recently learned, to maintain enslavement and to dissolve the country? He really wanted to know: *Why?*

Together, we talked about how these monuments had little to do with history; they were intended to reshape the world to come.

"Most of the people who were involved in erecting the monuments were not necessarily erecting a monument to the past," history professor Jane Dailey explains of the Confederacy revival movement, "but were rather erecting them toward a white supremacist future."

As narrative agents, memorials are bound up in problems of power. This never bothered me so much in the context of climate change, which seemed an absolute, affecting everyone. Wouldn't any narration of any version of the brutalities of climate change—its fact, its impacts—be fundamentally good? But this, too, is shaky ground. For as much as everyone on planet earth is vulnerable to climate change, we are unequally protected and exposed, and also unequally responsible. A memorial has the potential to speak to these facts or obscure them. As Bailey puts it in *In Memory Of*, "Every memorial comes with its own series of questions about how, why, what and/or whom we remember."

What tragedies are afforded memorials in the first place, and who decides? There are several hundred

Holocaust memorials worldwide, for instance, and yet only roughly a dozen memorials to enslavement in the United States. And while it's fruitless and even dangerous to rank the mass atrocities of the Holocaust and chattel slavery, it is all the same noteworthy that memory makers around the globe have privileged one over the other. Many longstanding memorials in the United States—the Jefferson Memorial, the Lincoln Memorial—are more figurative in form, built to honor only a certain version of the leader's life and legacy, and thus perpetuating that version at the exclusion of other truths about them less convenient to the act of memorializing (Jefferson as an enslaver, for instance, and Lincoln as the president who signed off on the largest mass lynching in U.S. history.) Such memorials, write the designers of a 2016 memorial competition entry, "attempt to tell us who we are by virtue of telling us who we were." But what about when they're hiding things?

There is also the problem of who is included in this designation of *we*, and who is doing the designating. For how can there possibly be a fixed, shared identity—past, present, or future—in such a nonmonolithic world? That is to say—how do we define the collective, and can such a thing even exist at scale? It's nearly impossible for a large population—residents of the United States, for instance—to agree on any version of the past, on what must be remembered and how. "As narratives unfold and splinter," writes architect David Adjaye, "there's almost a fracture—or even a certain failure—in the very idea of making memorials."

Other ethical quandaries of memorials are related to the process and mechanics of construction. Who is commissioning the memorial, who is designing it, and how is it being funded? At a Mexico City memorial to the victims of drug wars, the funding functioned as metaphor: because it was constructed using money seized from cartels, the politics of payment grafted to the memorial's overall purpose. At the same time, this particular memorial also reveals the trouble of collective memory. Some of the surviving family members felt excluded from the building process and incensed by the fact that no names were included in the memorial's design. After years of back and forth, the hulking bronze blocks are now shoddily affixed with laminated pages that list the names.

How to decide where a memorial gets built, and how it is (or isn't) designed in conversation with its surroundings? Is it situated in the exact place where an atrocity or loss occurred (the memorial at Auschwitz, for instance), or somewhere else, far away (there's a 9/11 memorial in India)? Bailey writes of the importance of a memorial structure "respectfully intervening" in the landscape. What is the effect of a memorial being large and announced, as with the 9/11 Memorial and Museum in New York, versus one more understated, like the memorial in Berlin to homosexuals persecuted and killed in the Holocaust— easy enough to walk by without even noticing?

It's no simple task, designing (or imagining, as the case may be) a memorial—even a memorial to the effects of climate change. And the stakes are high, since how we narrate the past can have a hand in writing the future.

5.

I poked around in search of the memory makers in the age of climate emergency—eager to immerse myself in its "industry of memory," in Thanh Nguyen's parlance. As nefarious as the industries of memory can be, and in spite of the pitfalls built into the very making of memorials, I continued to crave climate memorial spaces. Above all what I wanted was for us to remember the Earth as it once was by both cataloging and mourning the vanishings. "Until those whose memories are left out not only speak up for themselves but also seize control of the means of memory-making," Thanh Nguyen writes, "there will be no transformation in memory." How to allow a mass of land, a body of water, a species of bird, to speak?

In 2019, the writer Lacey Johnson traveled to the Okjökull glacier in Iceland—or, perhaps better put, the mound of earth formerly known as a glacier. The truth was, she writes, "Okjökull could no longer be classified as a glacier. It had become 'dead ice.'"

The ice on Ok glacier, as it was more commonly known, had been roughly seven hundred years old—and yet it had melted away in a matter of a few decades.

"A good friend has left us," a scientist said of its disappearance.

People in Iceland wanted to mark this loss like they would that of a loved one—for wasn't the glacier known and loved?—so one day, around a hundred gathered to hold a memorial. At the top of the former glacier, mourners read eulogies and shared memories. The scientist who discovered the very last of Ok's ice read what he called a death certificate, as if sharing an autopsy report.

"Its death was caused by excessive summer heat," he said. "Nothing was done to save it."

The world's glaciers are disappearing at a rapid pace—far faster, even, than many scientists had predicted. (The physics are such that the gush of melted water across the surface of a glacier only accelerates the melting.) The vanishing ice is certain to cause catastrophic sea level rise in coming years, destroying coastline communities and ecosystems and submerging entire islands.

But the melting glaciers are not only catastrophic in their physical effects. The death of a once-steadfast feature of the earthly landscape can unmoor the beings it left behind. As we watch the glaciers calve massive hunks of ice, we're witness to an extinction event, for soon enough, according to many predictive models, there may be no glaciers at all. In such a future, writes Andri Snær Magnason in *On Time and Water*, "Glaciers will be an alien phenomenon, rare as a Bengal tiger. Having lived in the time of the white giants will become swaddled in a fairy-tale glow, like having stroked a dragon or handled the eggs of the great auk."

Snær Magnason sees glaciers as "frozen manuscripts" that, like tree rings, have stories to tell about the past. This is a vanishing canon, a disappearing language—a storybook of the dead.

Death and loss are always, in part, abstractions. One moment a loved one is alive on this earth, and the next they simply are not. There is a helpful if disorienting finality associated with this sort of grief: a dead person, after all, is dead. So, too, with a glacier. But the uncertainty of our climate future—dependent on human action in the near and long term—makes the grief over it harder to reckon with, let alone transform.

In advance of Ok's memorial, mourners installed a plaque at the top of the former glacier onto which they'd inscribed a message to the future. They had asked Snær Magnason, a prominent local author, to write the text.

"It took me quite some time," he reflected later. "I wondered who I was addressing with the words on the plaque," he wrote. "I wondered at the absurdity of the task. How do you say goodbye to a glacier?"

Given the number of people who showed up to the memorial ceremony, it seems the notion of mourning a glacier—or any other casualty of the nonhuman world—wasn't so absurd after all. Even the prime minister of Iceland came to the ceremony. People were looking, like I was, for a sanctified space to mourn.

As the mourners gathered, the prime minister spoke solemnly into the crowed.

"The time has come not for words, not necessarily for declarations," she said, "but for action."

Words, words. "Ok is the first Icelandic glacier to lose its status as a glacier," Snær Magnason wrote upon the plaque. The eulogy spoke to both the present and the future. "In the next 200 years, all our glaciers are expected to follow the same path. This monument is to acknowledge that we know what is happening and what needs to be done. Only you know if we did it."

6.

Mnemosyne is the Greek goddess of Memory—a deity born before most of the other great gods of her pantheon, from a union of the Earth and the sky. It was Mnemosyne who gave birth to the nine muses, those creatures who proffer the gift of imagination to poets and to painters and to kings. Without memory, this mythic family tree suggests, there is no inspiration—no impulse to create.

Before the printing press and during times of widespread illiteracy, a sharp memory was critical for recounting stories in the oral traditions or, in the case of the rhetoric transitions of ancient Greece and Rome, presenting one's arguments in front of a crowd. In order to recall a long and complex text, many ancients would visualize a physical structure. The orator would construct a building in his mind with a clear picture of each room in the building and the order in which one moved through it. Each of the imagined rooms, called *loci*, would serve as the basis for a particular section of his speech. The orator—the architect of this imaginary space—would place a single object in each of the loci. When it came time to speak, he traveled through the palace in his mind's eye, room by room, "drawing from the memorized places the images he has placed on them," writes Frances Yates in *The Art of Memory*.

Architecture and memory have been in a long

cultural conversation—with the language of architecture serving as an ordering mechanism for the work of the mind, and memory influencing how and why we construct our physical world. "We shape our buildings," Winston Churchill famously said while imploring the House of Lords to rebuild the bombed House of Commons exactly as it had been before. "Thereafter they shape us." It's fitting, then, that we'd build physical structures to house our memory and grief.

7.

Heidi Quante of the Bureau of Linguistical Reality disagreed. "I don't know that we need any more buildings," she admonished gently when we finally connected by phone. The world had so many already—these static temples. She understood why I craved a space to enact memory and grief, but she was partial to the enactment itself—that is, to the power of ritual.

She explained that she was on her way up to Yosemite's Tuolumne Meadows that very afternoon, where she'd been working on a project related to the

Tuolumne River, which, due to dams and drought, is on the verge of environmental collapse. Quante spent her adulthood as an activist and community organizer, largely within the climate movement. This work, like much work that confronts systemic offenses, took its toll. When things felt bleak and smothering, she'd often jump into the Pacific. It would buoy her. But a few years back, she plunged into the sea and felt nothing.

"My depression didn't lift," she told me. "I knew I was fucked." Her friend invited her up to the mountains. When she stepped into the Tuolumne River, she said, felt like "one of those animals who'd been living in a cage their whole life and was finally let loose in the snow." She's returned to the river a couple times a year ever since for a dose of this alchemy.

She's now at work recording various elements of the river to, as she puts it, "help bring the water back to the people." Through immersive videos of three California rivers, gallery visitors can experience their healing power as well as grief over their imperilment.

Quante helped me see something I hadn't yet recognized: that, in yearning for a memorial related to climate grief, I was in part looking for a place to deposit it so I could leave it behind. *Cast your sorrows here . . .*

"Grief and sadness are not something to be edited out of life," she cautioned. What tends to be missing for many of us, she thinks, particularly those of us living in the U.S., are the rituals needed to metabolize these emotions. She sees this best done in connection with larger ecosystems in which we live. In creating a ceremony, she said, "you are holding a space for something to happen where someone can rest their bones or cry or reflect. For me it's less a building and more a space—a moment, or a magical pocket of time, to be held in that reflection." These grief spaces are necessarily ephemeral; time isn't just the subject matter, as with memorials, but the canvas.

"I just don't know that we need more buildings," she repeated.

I agreed with her in principle, but also felt that making a memorial manifest in the physical world— if even temporarily—was a central facet of my quest. When so many things were disappearing, risking being forgotten, I wanted to make something appear.

Time was running out on our conversation; I'd have to go soon, and Quante herself was due up in the mountains. So I turned to the matter of my word.

"Of course we can help with that," she said. But she couldn't just spit one out then and there. The way-finding of new language was a ritual unto itself, something that couldn't be rushed. But the following week, she told me, the Bureau of Linguistical Reality would be appearing at the Contemporary Jewish Museum and would be open for business—the nontransactional business of helping people create their words.

"I'll be there," I told her.

Not all built things were buildings, I supposed. And not all built things had to be permanent to offer meaning, to be of use.

8.

A young man in his twenties steps into the dwindling river. His hair is long, curls to his shoulders, and his feet are bare. He kneels down, scoops some water in his hands, and gets to work on his metropolis.

For the past few summers the young man has been coming to this place in Switzerland, not far from where he lives, to sculpt castles from the clay that lines the riverbank. In the summer, the water is lower, exposing the banks until the next rains. He shapes his castles with long turrets that bend like cypress trees and fix into points like wizard caps. He fashions parapets and gargoyles and wobbly bridges; over time he decides to sculpt a cathedral and walkways beneath a series of arches that bring to mind the gaping rib cages of dinosaurs. Every day he comes back to his riverbank, and every day his castle grows until it is no longer a castle anymore, but a fortress, and then a city—this steampunk apparition of mud.

Most years, he'd sculpt until the rains came and washed what he made away. That was part of the art-making—forming something ephemeral that in time would vanish with no trace. But this year there is no rain, and still no rain. His mud city grows and grows. Neighborhoods form, a history and iconography unfurl from the city like a scroll. He starts to imagine the people living in this world he has built. He can "see their world being created under [his] fingers."

Outside the walls of the city, the real Europe has been positively boiling; all summer the crops have wilted, fires have hurtled across the hillsides, and rivers, like this one, have been drying to mere trickles. A record number of people have died in the heat.

When you build a city of mud and dreams, you get to decide what happens there—what things mean and stand for, what the priorities are, what existential crises face this world and its people. Every day it failed to rain deepened the real world catastrophe but allowed the mud city to grow. It became more real with each scorching day—such that the artist began to mourn the fact that eventually the much-needed rain would come and wash it all away, making his creation riverbank again.

★★★

One of the promises of the early pandemic was that, by function of things being ground to a halt such that many people were forced to pay closer attention to the inequities and interconnectedness of things, we might actually rebuild unjust structures anew (healthcare, education, the social safety net). Of course it didn't happen that way. The world went on. No mud city, nor any other new universe, was built in the wreckage. COVID surged and retreated, surged and retreated again; the vaccines arrived; nonessential workers went back to work; Zoom meetings became real meetings. The hummingbirds Ben and I watched hatch during early COVID grew up, learned to fly, flew away. Wildfires tore through the state of California, the state of Oregon, the state of Washington—through Spain and Portugal and Canada and Greece. One day the sky above us was so clogged with smoke that everything was darkened, as if a curtain had been dropped from the sky. Some places flooded with sea swells and rushing rivers; in other places, like Switzerland, it failed to rain, the desiccated ground cracking open as if in desperate supplication. Along with these catastrophes came more grief still. And then, amid all of this, I became pregnant.

When we returned from Mexico, the memories of the dead fish stored on my phone, the baby continued to grow and time began to slow again. My sleep, usually untroubled, became a twilit experience. I often woke before dawn, lying in bed for hours but waiting to rouse myself until I heard the birds begin their morning songs.

Perhaps it was these long, taffy-like mornings that made me become more attuned to any birds other than our nesting hummingbirds. Until those wakeful, still-dark mornings, birdsong had been mere backdrop, sounds I barely noticed, not unlike the northbound train that rolled by in the middle of most nights, or the fire trucks hastening from their station around the corner.

Of course, this attunement led me down wormholes of destruction and doom: to be alive on today's planet is, as Daisy Hildyard writes, to hold two selves, to inhabit two bodies. "You have an individual body," she writes, "in which you exist, eat, sleep, and go about your day-to-day life. You also have a second body which has an impact on foreign countries and on whales." You can just be sitting somewhere in, say, Marseille, as she sees it, while your second body is "floating above a pharmaceutical plant on the outskirts of the city, it is inside a freight container on the docks, and it is also thousands of miles away, on a flood plain in Bangladesh, in another man's lungs." Essayist Elvia Wilk refers to this second body as "the ecosystem body," which both influences and is influenced by "ecologies beyond the individual self." We may or may not be aware of body number two, but the split is unavoidable, we inhabit both at once: the innocent and the implicated.

And what of the bodies that vanish? It's hard to parse how many of the world's birds have gone extinct. During early European colonization, settlers began overhunting the birds of the world for food and plumage and introducing invasive species that killed them off. Since then, at least 159 species have gone extinct worldwide—though some estimates are far higher. Right now, during the so-called "sixth extinction," the earth is experiencing a rapid species decline among all its creatures, not just the birds.

"We'll never get them back," the poet CAConrad said, words that trilled through my head for months like a mourning dove's call.

That spring, the days continued to warm, and I spent more and more of my time outside, nearer to the birds. Occasionally a hummingbird appeared, and I wondered if it was one of the ones I knew. "Hello," I'd call to it, "Hello, hello." Warm days in California felt precarious now—to be enjoyed but wary of, since fire seemed around the corner again. *Blissonance.* I learned around the thirtieth week of my pregnancy that my baby was starting to recognize sounds. I liked the thought that she was hearing all those birds through the protective membrane that separated her, for now, from the world—my flesh— and that, somehow, the sounds would be forever familiar to her, committed to memory.

Ben, meanwhile, began a more formal study of birdsong, downloading an app that helped him identify who was who. To him, the reservoir of undifferentiated sounds became a ravel of specifics: he could recognize individual voices within the scrum. In this way, he was learning a new language, attuned to an entirely new dimension of the world around us.

"The birds," I'd murmur in the early morning twilight when they began their calls.

"Towhee," he'd say, identifying the first bird to call before rolling over to go back to sleep. As the morning lightened, more would join the chorus. *House finch*, *song sparrow*, he'd mumble, occasionally *robin*. I'd try to commit them to memory, but always failed; by the next morning I'd awake as a blank slate again. *Towhee*, Ben would repeat from his half-slumber, *house finch*, *robin*.

★★★

Learning these languages seemed to come so easily for him: the language of the birdsong, but also the naming language that indexes them in the world.

That spring, I read Yoko Ogawa's novel *The Memory Police*, in which Ogawa renders an island where the ruling class is disappearing things—a cherry blossom, a pen, a kind of boat—and, along with the items, the islanders' memories. Physical dimensions of their world are, item by item, being erased. The islanders forget not just the object but its larger implications and function within the world. This reminded me of my disappearing words.

The weaponization of memory and the psychic peril of forgetting feature prominently in dystopic literature like *The Memory Police*, just as they do in dystopic corners of real-world society. In Orwell's *1984*, for instance, any incriminating document or contraband must be sent down the "memory hole."

"When one knew that any document was due for destruction, or even when one saw a scrap of waste paper lying about," Orwell wrote, "it was an automatic action to lift the flap of the nearest memory hole and drop it in, whereupon it would be whirled away on a current of warm air to the enormous furnaces which were hidden somewhere in the recesses of the building."

Dystopic stories are told to shine light on the structures and strictures within which we live. Through the defamiliarization of these off-kilter worlds, we are paradoxically better able to see our own. The fictional world of disappearances in *The Memory Police* is a clear corollary to the costs of climate change and our own age of disappearance: animal extinctions, mass tree die-offs, entire towns and landscapes drowned or burned. In the novel as in life, these disappearances change existence itself and chip away at humans' connections to place and their capacity to know and love one another.

Memorials might be fraught creatures, but all the same, remembrance can be an act against the tyrannical directive to forget. "Men who start by burning books," Ogawa writes, "end by burning other men."

The protagonist of *The Memory Police* discovers that her long-ago-disappeared mother had in fact been a cataloger of lost things. She had kept objects that had otherwise vanished off the island in a secret cabinet of drawers.

Much memory work involves a kind of catalog. The artist Elizabeth Turk, for instance, created what she called sound columns—ringed sculptures, some standing over eight feet tall, each shaped in the form of the sound wave of an extinct birdsong.

"I'm trying to give an absence   the huge number of extinctions in the natural world—physical form," Turk explained.

Similarly, in her project *Resurrecting the Sublime*, the artist Alexandra Daisy Ginsberg spent years researching extinct flowers in collaboration with synthetic biologists and paleogeneticists. They took DNA extracted from samples of extinct flowers and compared it to the genetic sequences of flowers that still grew on Earth, focusing on the species' olfactory profiles. In so doing, they were able to approximate the scents of the extinct flowers—resurrecting them, essentially, from the dead. Her team began to install human-sized dioramas in galleries, where visitors would enter, behold a landscape of the flower's former habitat, and be misted with the scent of its reincarnation, as if walking through the cosmetics department of a mall.

The fragrance, though based on science, was only an approximation.

"What we end up with is a blurry picture of the past, a false yet powerful memory," Ginsberg said. The experience gestured toward the possibility of tapping into primordial memory, reminding our most ancient self of flowers our predecessors might have smelled before, long ago.

For a brief period in 2022, *Songs of Disappearance: Australian Bird Calls*, an album compiled of the songs of fifty-three threatened Australian birds, beat out Taylor Swift's new record in the Australian charts. I listened to this album frequently over the course of that pregnant spring; some of the birds sang and trilled, others performed more of a honk or a police siren. This was the welcome backdrop in my home as I swept, cooked, typed, read, the rooms alive with the present vanishing.

One of the characters in *The Memory Police* is an old man who lives on a boat. He avoids talking politics at first, but over time, the character begins to see that, as Ogawa puts it, the island's disappearances were leaving the islanders with "hollow heart[s] full of holes."

"No matter how wonderful the memory," the old man says, "it vanishes if you leave it alone, if no one pays attention to it. They leave no trace, no evidence that they ever existed."

Catalogs can serve as antidotes to disappearance and as resurrections—but resurrection via memory can be a messy and incomplete business. "But I suppose you're right," the man continues, "when you say we should do everything we can to bring back memories of the things that have disappeared."

9.

According to Socrates, when the Egyptian god Thoth realized he had invented writing, he was so ecstatic that, as Socrates tells it, he raced to Thamus, the god-king, to boast of what he'd done.

"This invention, O king, will make the Egyptians wiser and will improve their memories; for it is an elixir of memory and wisdom I have discovered."

But Thamus wasn't impressed. This invention, he replied, was no good. Writing wasn't an elixir of wisdom and memory, he thought; quite the contrary: it would lead people to forgetfulness, because they would rely on what was written over what was remembered. "Their trust in writing," he said, "produced by external characters, which are not part of themselves, will discourage the use of their own memory within them."

Thamus was suggesting that memory was a muscle, one that writing would render feeble. Memory lives as if within the human skin, but writing is made of external stuff. "You have invented an elixir not of memory," he scolded, "but of reminding."

This legend spoke to me. I realized my problem with language wasn't just a matter of efficacy (wondering what good it did) or semantic satiation (losing track of what words even signified) but, perhaps most troubling of all, it was one of personal amnesia. I would read old articles and riffle through old notebooks to discover that a line I'd written recently was a verbatim copy of something I'd written long ago, that what felt like a recent epiphany wasn't one at all. Writing was supposed to help me remember what it was about the world that broke and moved me, but instead it felt powerless in the face of all I was trying to describe and even seemed to be making me forget, as the god-king warned.

Forgetfulness, in turn, gave way to further repetition, rendering words shopworn. (All those *vasts*: the vast desert, the vast sense of loss, the vast expanse of sky.) The writer Geoff Dyer points out that there's almost no writing about the so-called Great War—World War I—that doesn't mention the sweeping *horror* of it all—the time spent in the trenches, the piles and piles of bodies, all the young men shipped out to their certain deaths upon the (vast) battlefields. *Horror.* As Dyer writes in *The Missing of the Somme*, this word that attempts to offer clear meaning becomes, after so much repetition, meaningless. This is distinct from the feeling of semantic satiation, since it's not that we lose associative track of what words are supposed to mean, but that the overinsistence on a meaning becomes a diluting force. "Horror, on its own . . . ," he writes, "has no power to horrify. The more you pile it on like this, the faster linguistic wear proceeds." The word becomes stale, mere platitude, and can even serve as a numbing agent. "Strings of shuddering adjectives," he writes, "dull the reaction they are intended to induce."

As a writer chronicling human rights and environmental catastrophes, I had long grappled with this idea of linguistic wear: how not to obscure the issues or people or places I'm writing about with stagnant words. Though I found it painful to lack the language to describe the world, perhaps the stale words were, if feeble tools of meaning-making, strong doses of analgesic—distancing agents, like the photos of the fish and ice, keeping the unraveling of our planet in the realm of the platitude and the obscure rather than the vivid and the real.

"If one thing characterizes our time," writes Andri Snær Magnason, "it's the struggle over words, the power to define the world and its economy, the power to report and shape the news." Because words help determine the reality we live in, and how we see it, Magnason says, the true struggle "is about deciding how the world is worded."

In 2019, to stave off such mushiness of meaning and the attendant seepage of power, *The Guardian* updated its style guides with regard to environmental coverage. No longer would they be using *climate change* as the standard phrase but instead *climate emergency*, *climate crisis*, or *climate breakdown*. *Global heating* would be preferred over the term *global warming*; the distant scientific term of *biodiversity* would be scrapped for the more palpable *wildlife*. And no longer would the news organization talk of *climate skeptics*, but rather *climate science deniers*.

"We want to ensure that we are being scientifically precise, while also communicating clearly with readers on this very important issue," the outlet's editor in chief said in an article announcing the shift. "The phrase 'climate change,' for example, sounds rather passive and gentle when what scientists are talking about is a catastrophe for humanity." It was time to call things more directly as they were.

But the problem doesn't stop there. As the philosopher Glenn Albrecht put it, the planet is changing faster than our language is, and our retrograde lexicons don't adequately reflect either what is happening or how it makes us feel. Facing this absence, Albrecht (whom the Bureau cites as inspiration for their own work) has offered new language "to describe and 're-place' our emotions and feelings." His term *solastalgia*, for instance: the feeling of being homesick for the place where you are because you know that it is changing so quickly it will soon be rendered beyond recognition.

A further complication of the problem of language to describe our changing planet is that the languages humans have developed to describe the world are disappearing too. UNESCO has identified 8,324 languages on planet earth, and only 7,000 of these are still in use. Roughly half of those are in grave danger of soon disappearing. In quite literal terms, we have fewer words. However fallible language is, to lose a tongue means people are losing their mechanisms for knowing their history, their landscapes, their memories, themselves.

I once heard a radio story about the Turkish "bird language," a tongue of whistles and song used by farmers to communicate with one another across long distances in the hills where they lived and kept their animals. The whistle language allows a person to pass on information about the weather or the harvest, about a death and an upcoming funeral, and can even share a phone number across the hilly green.

"The only thing you never whistle is your love talk," a woman named Cakir told the journalist interviewing her, "Because you'll get caught!"

The whistle language was always a minority language—a communication system evolved to suit the needs and desires of a particular community living on a particular landscape. Its vanishing is a function of its irrelevancy. Everyone has cell phones now. Who needs to whistle across long distances when you can just text?

So my crisis of language and memory wasn't occurring in a vacuum. We did indeed urgently need, like Albrecht and the Bureau argued, new methods of rendering the global crisis, and new words.

10.

Over years of traveling to Slovenia, I got to know an architect named Janko Rosic. He was in his twenties when he was conscripted into the Yugoslav army. He'd had no interest in the war, he told me, in the kind of nationalism it stoked. He was an artist, not a warrior; he believed in cultivating life, not death. At night, after his trainings, cast in the low light of the rationed candles, he and some other artists would get together and talk philosophy, dreams—these antitheses of war. They gave themselves a name too: Sestava, or cell. It was a word with a lot of power, in part because it meant two things at once: a cell like a prison cell, a cell like in biology. They'd named themselves for their feeling of entrapment in the army and also for the smallest unit of life.

In 1991, Slovenia finally declared independence from Yugoslavia after years of rule under other regimes: the Italians, the Nazis, the Austro-Hungarian Empire. They weren't in Yugoslavia anymore; now this was Slovenia.

Independent Slovenia was one largely filled with optimism for the future. It was also one mired in capitalist scramble. One of the new government's first acts was to "modernize" the brutalist city, bringing capitalist commerce front and center where socialism had once reigned. Just east of the Ljubljanica River, the city's flowing heart, the Metelkova district had long been the local command center for whatever ruling power controlled Slovenia at the time. Passed from occupying regime to occupying regime, Metelkova was like an heirloom of totalitarian rule, comprised of army barracks, prison blocks, and places to hitch the horses. This was the place where perceived enemies of whatever regime held power were thrown into solitary confinement, locked up for crimes both real and imagined—where they were tortured, shot, slain.

The post-independence modernization plans called for Metelkova to be razed in order to build a mall and parking lots. Janko and his friends from Sestava were outraged. They would destroy this hallowed place—for a mall?

"To destroy a place like Metelkova was to destroy its history," Janko felt, and erase the memories of what took place there. Many agreed. The area quickly became a squat for young artists, freethinkers, and political radicals, as well as drug addicts and youth in search of a cause, all of whom had come of age in a time of political repression during which the specter of Metalkova, and of imprisonment for dissent, loomed large. Janko and the Sestava collective joined the squatters, while the new government proceeded with its plans. The night before Metelkova's main prison was to be smashed to bits, nearly two hundred people jumped the wall and occupied the building.

"The next day, we stopped the bulldozers with our bodies," Janko recalled. The prison, along with the rest of Metelkova, was saved.

But they wanted to do something with it, not just keep it until it fell to ruin. But what would they make of this haunted space they'd wrested from destruction?

They imagined building the entirety of Metelkova into the artistic center of Ljubljana, and somehow creating a living memorial of the casualties of pre-independence violence in Slovenia. It was a good idea but mostly theoretical. For weeks, they deliberated about what form this might take in the actual world.

"We wanted to create an open space, a space that was the opposite of a prison," Janko recalled of Sestava. It was wordplay again. What is the *opposite* of a prison? Eventually, they came to an answer—an unlikely one, as memorial spaces go. They would build a hostel, a place where people from across Europe, across the world, would be free to come and go.

In 2003, they opened Celica. They refashioned the first floor to be airy and bright and fashioned the excavator wound into a window. They built a front door of wood and glass such that it functioned as a sundial, casting a pillar of light down the hallway at exactly noon each solstice. Structurally, they kept the two floors of small cells as they were but invited artists and art collectives from around the world to redesign them. For over a century, prisoners of that long line of regimes had packed into these small cells, sometimes as many as ten or twelve men, so cramped they had to sleep on their sides arranged head to toe along the floor. They died of exposure, of disease, of malnutrition, of heartbreak, and were executed outside in broad daylight. Each artist was assigned a cell, and their project was to turn it from a closed, cramped space of confinement into one of beauty, and freedom.

During the annual writers' residency in Slovenia, I'd take students to visit Celica so we could study the way stories could be told through a physical space in hopes that this would help us see our written work anew. Janko always gave our group a tour, showing us the sundial; the second floor's prayer room; how the first floor was modeled after a Roman agora; the way the floors upstairs sloped slightly downward, to mimic the feeling of lightness of that first step toward freedom. We'd also visit a number of the transformed cells, seeing how each artist had responded to the project of opening a place of repression into one of freedom, space, and light. Each room had a regular door but also a gate, evocative of a prison cell. How do we transform something, I wondered on each visit, without forsaking or lampooning the past?

★★★

Janko introduced me to a man named Peter Romavh who had been detained in Metelkova as a young boy.

By 1942, as war swept Europe, the Italian Fascists had encircled all of Ljubljana with a glinting ring of razor wire: no one in, no one out. The streets were peopled with soldiers and secret police. Peter's father was a municipal railway worker and member of the underground Communist Party organizing against the Fascist occupation, and as such he avoided speaking to others in public—even to those he knew—lest he be discovered. Ljubljana was in effect a highly controlled municipal prison, guarded by Fascist soldiers in their green felt uniforms and polished knee-high boots.

Though leaving Ljubljana was nearly impossible for most ordinary citizens, the freedom fighters' link to the railway provided an easy pipeline out of the city through which they could deliver messages and disseminate liberation ideology through the occupied territories. To counter their efforts, the Triple Alliance demanded that any such resistance fighters be captured and killed.

When Peter was just six years old, the soldiers stopped Peter's father in the streets. They searched him and found liberation literature stuffed into his coat pocket. He was taken straight to prison in Metelkova, next to the barracks that became Celica. Ten days later, just before six-year-old Peter was scheduled to start kindergarten, armed guards dragged mother and son into a women and children's ward at what is now Celica—the hostel where I was sleeping.

There, Peter's mother was interrogated and beaten for information about her husband's activities. But she knew few details, and she refused to cede whatever knowledge she did have. They were aware that Peter's father was imprisoned just across the courtyard, packed into a room full of hostages all awaiting near-certain execution. "Everyone who stayed there knew that he would be shot," Peter said.

During the Second World War, over 100,000 Slovenes were killed out of a population of approximately one million, which made it, percentage-wise, the second largest casualty center in all of Europe. During this time, over 2,500 hostages were executed— often publicly—on Lubljana's cobbled streets. Every Ljubljanan of that era, Peter told me, had witnessed an execution.

After several months, Peter and his mother were released but found their home had been looted of all its possessions. His father, however, remained in prison. After a few weeks of freedom, he and his mother heard five concise gunshots puncture the morning air. Somehow they knew that the sounds meant that Peter's father was dead.

★★★

One summer, after the residency was over, I decided to stay a few nights at Celica in hopes of writing about it. By then, Celica had been voted Europe's hippest hostel by Lonely Planet multiple times. Was this success or desecration? I got my keys at the front desk while a bunch of rowdy Brits drank beer in the courtyard then walked upstairs. The artists who designed my room had reimagined it as a giant eye: the circular bed, like the room's somber iris, was lofted in the center and accessed by a spiral ladder: an optic nerve. Paintings of eyes of many sizes covered the walls as though depicting animals lurking in the dark.

My window faced the courtyard where the city's counterculture kids came to party, outlasting the night into morning. "We built this hostel to transform the deeds of the past into a new light," Janko had explained. How do we simultaneously honor the dead, make space for grief, and also hold space for life—all that partying on the street, for instance—and for the future? A hostel had felt like a silly answer when I first learned of it, not only a prison's sloppy inverse but an irreverent memorial. Over time I had come to appreciate the earnestness of the vision, its idealism and its bombast—and its belief in the possibility of true transformation.

"What are you writing about?" one of the founding members of Sestava asked me over beers one night in Celica's courtyard as we waited for the others. I explained I was writing about Celica, about its history, about the conundrum of memorial-building.

"Ah, you are interested in memory," she said.

It had been over twenty years since the war and the first imagining of Celica, and five founding members of Sestava now gathered in the courtyard to speak to me about the past.

What did they remember of their military service, I wondered.

"The smell," they said, in almost unanimity. The odor of the barracks, of the men, of the uniforms—as if the scent of war itself. You could smell it when you fell asleep at night, during mealtime, after a smoke or a rare shower, in the hot months when they boiled while marching and while sleeping, but also in the cold months too. I was after stories of war, a narrative, but what they remembered was, like the olfactory inverse of a field of flowers gone extinct, the wretched smell.

We went inside to look again at the space they had created. That summer, a visiting artist from Vienna was working on an installation in the building's dungeon, and they wanted me to see it.

At the end of the central hallway stood a small, unassuming staircase. Each step downward was a descent into the past. The dungeon was pitch black and musty. Behind the staircase were two small stone rooms—solitary confinement cells.

"Completely closed spaces," Janko said, "where people were deprived not only of freedom, but also of light."

The Viennese artist had fashioned a tiny seed out of gold—no bigger than a kernel of rice—which she was going to place upon the stones in a former cell. A visitor would be hard pressed to find it but would know it was there, this valuable contrivance pulsing somewhere in the dark.

This was my favorite part of Celica: underground. The dungeon was the only part that hadn't been renovated because, as Janko explained, "we wanted to keep this place as it was, to speak for itself."

But there was one small exception. In time, one's eyes adjust to the basement, and notice a thin ray of light emerging from a tiny hole in the stone. If you turn toward the back wall, you can watch the goings-on of the Metelkova courtyard outside, flipped upside down. The Sestava team had drilled this hole to fashion it into a camera obscura. We watched quietly as people in the former prison courtyard walked by, locked up their bikes, chatted with one another, were free.

Memorial spaces needn't just be places to feel sorrow, I understood, but possibility, life. "This," said Janko of the camera obscura, "is our invitation from darkness."

11.

When the Slovene poet Tomaž Šalamun was dying, his wife, the painter Metka Krašovec, arranged for an artist friend to cast his death mask. She arrived to their flat one afternoon with the necessary materials and began wetting strips of plaster in a bowl by his bed. One by one, she gently laid them across Šalamun's face until it was completely covered. Once the material had dried, the artist peeled back the mask. Metka looked at Tomaž. Face uncovered now, the poet, hovering between this world and whatever would come next, was smiling.

"Tomaž was happy!" Krašovec recalled to me over dinner one night, clapping her hands.

By then he was long gone, but Metka still had the mask—a physical object that marked the threshold days of his passing. Death masks were a common ritual across ancient traditions—from Egypt to the Arctic to Southeast Asia. In some cases, the mask was left with the living, and sometimes even worn by mourners during funeral rites. In other cases, the deceased person was buried with the mask to ensure that the spirit would be recognized in the afterworld, or to ward off evil. The practice was revived in the seventeenth century, largely for powerful tyrants like Napoleon and Alexander I, but with the advent of photography, the practice of death masks faded from use once again.

Metka had turned to an old, out-of-fashion ritual, adapting it to her own purposes as she grieved her husband's passing and prepared to say goodbye.

Humans have always struggled to make sense of death. Many societies, from Finland to Greece to Guatemala, created dedicated roles in the community for grieving—outsourcing, as it were, the grief to professionals who sobbed laments for the dead. These cries were acknowledgments of the individual being mourned and also wails of the collective; they served as a sonic bridge between this world and the spirit world hereafter.

Rituals exist to support us through rites of passage—birth, death, menstruation, marriage—and through the difficulties endemic to living. A repeated cultural practice reminds us that many before us have passed through these same gates of joy or celebration or sorrow and managed to keep on living.

"Ritual is a very ancient social technology," explains cognitive anthropologist Dimitris Xygalatas, "and it fulfills the exact same roles today as it did for our ancestors thousands of years ago." Only today, as Quante had pointed out, much of modern society is void of ritual. Who has time? Grief rituals are, like the world's languages and so many species of birds, becoming endangered and going extinct.

Would it be possible to create a life mask of an endangered species of bird? Do we need to revive the role of lament singer? The power of such rituals is that they help us access a sorrow that is at once before and beyond language and enact it through the body itself.

★★★

The poet CAConrad awakens at daylight in a Walmart parking lot, where they've spent the night. They exit the car, place a speaker at their feet, and hit play. The calls of the now-extinct Hawai'i 'ō'ō bird begin and reverberate up their body, bathing Conrad in these sounds of an animal lost to time. They begin walking in spiral formation until they enter something of a trancelike state, and then they walk through the Walmart's front doors. Conrad considers each Walmart a "massive indoor city" that mars this country's landscape, each hardly distinguishable from the next, and all hallmarks of contemporary waste, capital, and greed.

Once inside the "Walmart Dimension," speaker in hand and cloaked in the 'ō'ō's calls, Conrad sits down in one of the aisles (seated, they are generally permitted to stay; it's when they lie down that an employee tries to kick them out) and begins to channel language. *Take our time studying trees, to imagine the nest we would build if we were birds.* These words will become poems—conducted, like electricity, from the vibrational sounds of species that will never return. *All I have ever wanted was to forge the English language into a spear and shove it into my heart.*

This is Conrad's *Resurrect Extinct Vibration*, a poetry ritual that they repeated at Walmarts throughout the country. It created an atmosphere of exaltation amid the debasement of Walmart. *We don't need more buildings.* We certainly don't need more Walmarts.

When a species disappears, Conrad says, "the gossamer of this world that holds all that life together breaks down." What are memorials but gossamers woven anew from the broken, lost things—bones, riverbanks, birdsongs—and our memories of what those things were and what they stood for?

Speaking with the critic David Naimon, Conrad explains that inside the massive hubbub of Walmart, "I would be filling my body with the sounds of these extinct animals, and I was enjoying it, and I found that disturbing." There was a sense of exuberance from these sounds that didn't square with their extinction. But they also understood that these sounds were resonant on an almost cellular level. Our cells, in Conrad's estimation, hold memories of vibratory frequencies from long, long ago—from generations before us and many generations before that, as if the sounds of these dead creatures were stored somewhere in our DNA like ancestral memories.

During the interview, Naimon shared a recording of the extinct Hawai'i 'ō'ō. The bird's call was echoey and mournful, as if emitted from a dripping underwater cave; it sounded less like a bird and more like a conjuring flute from a distant world. I was driving on the highway as I listened, and was so moved by this song that I nearly had to pull onto the shoulder to steady myself. Conrad explained that though the sounds were pleasantly altering when one was immersed in them, the aftermath—reentering the world in which those sounds no longer existed—left them billowed in grief.

Later, yearning to hear the call again, I searched for a video of the Hawaiʻi ʻōʻō online. It was a small black bird with yellow tufted wings whose beak curved like a scythe and whose long tail fell behind it like a bridal train. In the video, the ʻōʻō stands in a forest, tilts its head, and issues a call through the trees. It listens, hears nothing, and calls again—and again, and again. It's waiting for a reply but won't find one. For this, it seems, is the last Hawaiʻi ʻōʻō in the world.

★★★

A year after his death, I asked Metka how she was faring without Tomaž.

"It's harder now," she said, than it was after he first died. She still missed him terribly, and yet the collective rituals and celebrations surrounding his death had mostly passed. Now, it was just her in an empty house. "It's tiresome to eat alone at restaurants so often," she told me. What she was really saying was, "It's tiresome to be so alone with my grief." There was no ritual to mark this period of time, which made it all the more cavernous and lonely. Of their somatic poetry rituals, Conrad said, "These rituals also help us not be so alienated from one another and from the planet." If grief is a condition of estrangement, ritual is an enactment of relation.

12.

Though often cited as such, it's clear that language is not what separates humans from nonhuman animals. In fact, "what best distinguishes our species," writes psychologists Martin E. P. Seligman and John Tierney, "is an ability that scientists are just beginning to appreciate: we contemplate the future." A preparation for and imagination of a vague tomorrow is what first propelled our ancestors to plant crops, to build cities and apiaries and aqueducts and airplanes. Not unlike Halbwachs speaking of memory, Seligman and Tierney write that the future is a "jointly constructed" feature of our species. A future focus also serves the biological function of perpetuating the human race.

But in times of strife—and particularly during this era of ecological collapse and mass destruction— imagining the future can plunge a person, or even entire communities, into a state of depression. This is a rather rational response, as Wray explains in *Generation Dread*, because however unknowable the particulars of the future may be, what we do know is that, even in the best of circumstances, great devastation is to come. More fires will swallow up our hillsides, more sweltering summers will suffocate people in the fields and in their homes, more inches and even feet of sea-level rise will choke out ecosystems and drown houses, more tropical storms will ravage our landscapes, more droughts will leave people and animals gasping with thirst.

★★★

I was familiar with spirals of apocalyptic thought— they were what had brought me to my memorial quest, after all. But I also recognized in them the potential for an endless loop. In *Not Too Late*, writer and activist Rebecca Solnit posits that "a lot of stories in circulation endeavor to strip you of hope and power, to tell you it doesn't matter or it's too late or there's nothing you can do or we can never win." Alive as climate grief is among so many of us, an overfocus on grief at the expense of current and future positive change can serve as an immobilizer, and even a form of solipsism. It can become all about what's already happened rather than what's still possible, and it can become all about *me*: my grief, my feelings—my world.

"We believe that the truths about the science, the justice-centered solutions, the growing strength of the climate movement and its achievements can help," Solnit and her *Not Too Late* coeditor, Thelma Young Lutunatabua, write. "They can assuage the sorrow and despair, and they can help people see why it's worth doing the work the climate crisis demands of us." We can feel sorrow and despair while also remembering, as Solnit writes, "our own heroic nature, our capacity for courage, compassion, and action," as well as all the people "who came before us and took action against the odds and sometimes won."

"If we succeed in defeating the fossil fuel industry," Solnit writes elsewhere, "those who come after will look back on the age of fossil fuel as an age of corruption and poison. The grandchildren of those who are young now will hear horror stories about how people once burned great mountains of poisonous stuff dug up from deep underground that made children sick and birds die and the air filthy and the planet heat up."

Grief, in other words, needn't be a terminus but a portal.

★★★

It turns out that even in this era of mass destruction, when merely thinking about the future can plunge us into despair, *planning* for the future tends to make humans happy. A recent study showed that most people think about the future three times more often than the past, explain Seligman and Tierney. "When making plans, they reported higher levels of happiness and lower levels of stress than at other times, presumably because planning turns a chaotic mass of concerns into an organized sequence." To plan toward the future is to believe that good memories lie in wait up ahead.

So it is to design the future world. "At its core," writes Nikil Saval, "design is an inherently futurist medium." Design was once a largely optimistic pursuit—ecstatic, even, for designers were both imagining what the future needed and bringing that future into being. (Saval recounts designer Charles Eames's response to the question posed to him in 1969, "What are the boundaries of design?": "What are the boundaries of problems?" was his reply.) But Saval explains that all large-scale design must now grapple with a new existential question: "How do you design for the future when the future you are designing for will not exist?"

This poses a double problem: designers must simultaneously anticipate an unanticipatable future and design protective solutions in service of that world. This is imagination work, the futurist Johanna Hoffman explains, for "imagination massages the spaces between what could be and what is, transforming future uncertainties and hopes into present-day choices."

In 2017, the United Arab Emirates commissioned a design firm called the Future Energy Lab to redesign its cities in light of the looming climatic shifts that will dramatically affect the country's landscape, economy, and daily life. The firm constructed a "model metropolis" based on predictions of the city's future environment. This metropolis was a simulation of sorts, nesting five potential futures within a single immersive exhibition—each future a result of different policy decisions made in the near term. "The scenarios varied at many detailed levels: implementation of renewable energy technologies, alternate public transport networks, peer-to-peer energy trading, as well as social and cultural shifts," the designers explained. When the exhibit opened, visitors—mostly government officials—arrived to each simulation as though ghosts moving through a Dickensian dream. They were shown a broad range of metrics, like happiness indexes and neighborhood affordability, as well as more visceral, immersive insights into the future. For instance, in what the firm named the "business as usual" scenario—in which no changes were made to current emissions or policies—visitors bent over to examine a series of small plastic tubes containing samples of air reflecting the city's projected pollution levels in the years 2020, 2028, 2034. "It was noxious stuff," the designers wrote, "impossible to inhale even a small amount."

These projected UAE futures weren't abstractions. "These were not objects of prophesy, but of potential," the designers wrote. Their job had been to facilitate a direct, clear-eyed encounter with the future that at the same time gave their clients "a means to work with [it]."

Akin to what Solnit and Lutunatabua have identified in various corners of the climate movement is "dystopian dominance," which futurist Johanna Hoffman laments as a problem in the design field. "When existing visions of the future skew so heavily apocalyptic," she writes, "adaptive planning becomes more difficult to achieve." But if we want to avoid a landscape of toxic air in twenty years' time, designers need to offer policymakers tangible options for a future in which we can breathe. By creating an element of choice within their design scenarios, the Future Energy Lab endowed the UAE policymakers with a sense of urgent agency—the power to choose, in effect, away from dystopia, to choose life.

Not all futurist designs are as pragmatic as the Future Energy Lab project. In fact, many futurist designs are more provocation than plan—speculative, notional blueprints that nonetheless help push policy-oriented thinking, as well as public imagination, into new, generative realms. Hoffman cites Eneropa as an example—a proposition that, to render Europe carbon-neutral by 2050, entirely redrew the map of Europe's internal borders, creating altogether new states whose borders were drawn according to their renewable energy capacities.

Of course, the design wasn't implemented—but that hadn't really been the goal. "Rather than an idealized, achievable utopia," Hoffman writes, the designers "presented the venture more along the lines of, 'What do you think of this out-there idea?'" The out-there-ness of the idea forced conversation among legislators and within the general public of regional renewability and the prospect of a shared grid throughout Europe (funneling energy from the north's winter winds toward the south in the darker months, then routing the south's solar energy northward during summer) into the foreground. Such world building provocations, as Hoffman puts it, have the power to elicit questions "until the questions outline a story with shape, nuance and scale."

One of the most terrifying aspects of climate change is how amorphous it renders the future. Futurists are interested in how we design the world to come, but, like me, they also seem to grapple with questions of language. What is the spatial language of the future, and how do we speak of it not only in terms of doom but with the vocabulary of imagination and play?

A firm called Superflux creates designs for a future world in which humans can survive climate catastrophe and mediate its effects—models for a future seabed where seaweed harvesting has rebalanced the pH of the sea, for instance, or for a sustainable water grid for Mexico City. "Blending critical foresight with speculative and experiential design approaches," writes Superflux, "allow[s] us to transform data-heavy projects into poetic and affecting experiences." The notion that a physical space could provide something akin to poetry—that's what I was after in my study of memorial.

Memorials are forms of spatial storytelling about the past, but they can also be mandates to face the future and attempt its ethical redesign. Futurist designs, conversely, are focused on the world we do not yet inhabit, which cannot be imagined or designed for without a thorough examination of the past—past policies, past technologies, past styles and forms and civilizations and ways of life.

By the time I'd started studying futurism, my definition of *memorial* had morphed and stretched. The futurist designs seemed to attend to present grief over what has already been destroyed, as well as the vague but certain destruction to come, by offering the vivid portrait of a place to take up residence—a place to live—determined by sustainable interventions and solutions that staved off doom.

I visited a design firm in San Francisco called the Future Cities Lab, now Future Forms, which dreamed up a new vision for the San Francisco waterfront in an age of sea-level rise. Their model was at once enchanting and practical. I liked its optimism for my home city: namely, that if my house becomes a permanent fixture of the bay floor, I don't have to sink along with it—that there still might be a city, and that it could in fact be a lovely place to live in spite of its unsettling topographic revisions.

The Future Cities Lab was housed in a large postindustrial building in the southeastern swath of San Francisco. On the day I visited, 3D printers toiled away while human designers fit the robot-made pieces together and tested mechanics on a large square table strewn with rulers and power tools. Above the entrance hung a model of the Bay Bridge, underneath which dangled lush airborne islands. Not too long from now, lab cofounder Jason Kelly Johnson explained to me, the west section of the Bay Bridge will need to be rebuilt. What if the bridge housed colonies of displaced people who could farm and fish and self-sustain? Thick ribbons would raise and lower the small islands according to the time of day and the weather—lower if it's too windy, higher to get better views and shade. These ribbons also harvested fog, turning the vapor into water for agriculture and for drinking.

"It's not about solving climate change anymore," Kelly Johnson told me, "it's about dealing with it."

The current and approaching environmental apocalypse—and attendant grief—presents an opportunity to both accommodate the changing environment and create more symbiotic living arrangements, the sort that might have staved off some of this collapse in the first place. But such futures needn't be purely utilitarian in form. Their designs are compelling and smart, but what drew me to the Future Cities Lab was their vision of a new world of environmental cooperation that is also beautiful and moving—like a memorial is—and depicted a place where I'd actually like to live.

After visiting the lab I drove home across the west section of the Bay Bridge. I imagined living on one of their suspended pods of earth hovering between the bridge and the water, between the obsolete product of man and the sustaining, threatening sea. That's where we are now, isn't it. Dangling between the landscape and human folly, deciding what to do about the future as it shapes and reshapes itself and us before our very eyes.

13.

"The only recognizable feature of hope is action," the writer Grace Paley said. Of the climate crisis, activist Greta Thunberg implores, "I want you to act. I want you to act as you would in a crisis. I want you to act as if the house is on fire, because it is."

Because oft-repeated words lose their power, even these urgent demands for action can also become numbing agents. As a writer, I knew that words could sometimes feel like not only the antithesis of action, but also, worse, like mechanisms of concealment for doing nothing at all: empty gestures in the mouths of politicians, static social media slogans, platitudes on memorial plaques—*never again, in memory of, may we never forget.* I wanted for change to be made manifest in the world, and I continued to doubt my, or anyone's, ability to manage that with words.

There was also the matter of limited time. How could I maximize my life's concrete impact?

Submerged in endless deadlines and juggling various jobs at once, I was living a life that was perpetually antsy and hurried, which could get in the way of channeling my energies to the highest and best good. Yet the fate of the world did in fact depend on haste, and I also had the looming deadline of a baby being born. I had spent so much time thinking, reading, worrying, writing. What should I *do*?

★★★

When I met him in Slovenia, Peter Romavh, by then an old man, had recounted to me how, even after his father was plucked from the prison that is now Celica and executed in broad daylight, the treason charge followed the family like a hex. Peter and his mother were barred from accessing the regime-issued ration cards, and since the city was walled off from the rest of the world, there were scarce other sources of food. They were forced to scrounge and bargain. In springtime, they filled their garden with potatoes and carrots and greens and raised rabbits to skewer and roast. Next door, a better-off family kept a team of goats. They hired Peter to herd them toward the grassy outskirts of town to graze, near the barbed border where soldiers stood watch. He did this work in exchange for milk. Peter and his mother also secured counterfeit ration cards which they then sold to others for a good price. Like this, they physically survived the Italian occupation.

As a form of spiritual survival, young Peter would hide rusted nails under the tires of military vehicles. His father was dead, but his home became a hub for the underground network of freedom fighters yet again. They relied upon neighborhood boys like Peter to deliver notes on bicycle from one home to another, which they rolled like tiny scrolls and stashed in the hollows of their handlebars.

In the name of his murdered father, the little boy took action. "This was our obligation," Peter told me of his band of small liberators. This was his resistance work, his imagination work, his work as a futurist— each action a gesture of memorial in his father's name.

★★★

As I continued my grief-stricken inquiry into memorials, I began to notice a pattern in those that drew me most, what I came to think of as active memorials: memorials that not only ask visitors to move through them and be moved by them but that are themselves forms of action—memorials that actually move.

In her poem "38," Layli Long Soldier writes of the December 26, 1862, hanging of thirty-eight Lakota men in Minnesota—the largest mass execution in United States history. "The hanging took place on December 26, 1862—the day after Christmas," she writes. "This was the *same week* that President Lincoln signed the Emancipation / Proclamation."

Every year in the wake of this massacre, she writes:

The Memorial Riders travel 325 miles on horseback for eighteen days, sometimes through subzero blizzards.

They conclude their journey on December 26, the day of the hanging.

Memorials help focus our memory on particular people or events.

Often, memorials come in the forms of plaques, statues, or gravestones.

The memorial for the Dakota 38 is not an object inscribed with words, but an act.

Why must a memorial be still, bolted to the ground, fixed in place? I think this is what Quante, of the Bureau of Linguistical Reality, had been trying to make me see. The active movement of a memorial in the physical world maps to the experience of being emotionally moved—not in the sense of having merely felt something, but having been, through experience, made different, transformed.

Another such memorial: In 2020, in an attempt to mark the losses during COVID's first year, the artist Jill Magid engraved 120,000 pennies with the words *The body was already so fragile.* These 120,000 pennies added up to the amount of a single federal stimulus check. She began doling out the coins around New York City, where they continued to circulate.

"The idea," wrote Jillian Steinhauer in *The New York Times*, "was to make people think about the connections between economic and social conditions: The coins spread through human interaction, like the virus, and *the body* could refer to the physical ones or to an already vulnerable body politic." The unassuming memorial coins passed from hand to hand like tiny copper emissaries.

A memorial often attempts to help visitors conceive of the scale of what's been lost—a pile of shoes

at the U.S. Holocaust Memorial Museum, for instance, or a stack of skulls displayed at the Choeung
Ek Genocidal Center in Cambodia. In 2021 and
2022, more than 4,000 children were killed by gun
violence in the United States—a number that, like
most such statistics, is at once staggering and obscure. So in the summer of 2022, a group of parents
and activists built what they called the NRA Children's Museum: lined up, this caravan of fifty-two
empty school buses stretched over a mile long and
held enough seats for the more than 4,000 dead
children. This was a caravan of ghosts. In the wake
of the Uvalde school shooting, the NRA Children's Museum stationed itself outside of Senator
Ted Cruz's office in downtown Houston in protest
of his gun policies and his chart-topping funding
from the NRA. Idling there in front of his offices,
the buses were a clarity of scale, an insistent memorial to the dead, an accusation, and a demand for a
different world.

★★★

As Long Soldier references, these memorials in
action—akin to ritual—stand in stark contrast to

figurative monuments, those static statues, those "objects inscribed with words," whose primary projects are to valorize and cement a set of facts into stone.

The multimedia artist Nicholas Galanin takes up monuments as a subject and makes moving art of their toppling. As part of the 23rd Biennale of Sydney, he created "Shadow on the Land, an Excavation and Bush Burial." He dug a tidy hole in the ground in the exact shape of the shadow cast by the monument of Captain Cook that stands in a central Sydney park. Cook, like many colonizers, remains a lionized figure in Australian history books, in spite of the Indigenous genocide, theft, and ecological destruction he facilitated and represents. This design invites the viewer to imagine pushing the monument over into its hole.

"Inverting the gaze of archaeology," Galanin writes, "which has often framed Indigenous cultures as belonging to the past, this work imagines a possible future where the memories of settler colonialism have become distant and buried."

Galanin completed a similar installation at Davidson College in North Carolina. In the garden that once belonged to the home of the college

president—a garden long tended by enslaved people—Galanin and collaborators excavated the silhou-
ette of Andrew Jackson's statue in Washington, D.C.
Jackson had deep ties throughout the South and was
also a primary architect of Indigenous exclusion and
genocide; by dispossessing Indigenous people of
their ancestral lands, which were also legally theirs
in the language of U.S. treaty, Jackson, as the exhibition notes describe, "opened twenty-three million
acres of the cotton belt to plantation agriculture and
chattel slavery." Here in this former garden, his legacy and monument are being symbolically buried in
his own form.

But this is not just a work of toppling. The space
will be tended toward new life. In collaboration
with local Catawba tribal members and their food
sovereignty project, Galanin planted heirloom Catawba corn within the perimeter of Jackson's silhou-
etted hole. This corn nearly went extinct as a result
of forced displacement and industrial agriculture but
was saved by the seedbanks of the Catawba tribes.
Over time, the corn they planted will sprout and
grow until it obscures the excavation, overtaking
Jackson's form. They'll harvest it, Galanin said, "and
then we will feast."

***

When our school group traveled to Montgomery, we visited the National Memorial for Peace and Justice. Unlike the static, incomplete, dead-eyed story proffered by the Confederate monument, this memorial, we found, combined elements of traditional monuments, figurative and abstracted memorials, and memorials that moved.

We entered through a wide, grassy garden, past statues of men and women bound in chains. The pathway led us slightly uphill into a covered outdoor hall, where a collection of copper boxes resembling upright coffins were suspended from above. Each box was inscribed with a county and state, and a list of names: the list of all known lynchings of Black people that had been committed there.

While at first glance this memorial took the form of "plaques, statues, or gravestones," as Long Soldier had put it, there was also something staggering in their cumulative effect. Row after row, upright coffin after upright coffin, name after name after name. As we walked on, the ground began to slope downward, the coffins lifting toward the sky above the path—as if spirits ascending toward the heavens, but also as if bodies being hung. They dangled above us, these heavy metal chests; it was at once stirring and frightening to walk beneath their great physical and metaphoric weight.

At the bottom of the slope was a wide wall over which a thin, continuous stream of water fell, as if to offer cleansing. "Thousands of African Americans are unknown victims of racial terror lynchings whose deaths cannot be documented," read the script upon the wall, "many whose names will never be known. They are all honored here."

Soon, the memorial opened back up to the green: a breath again. Here, another collection of coffins was laid out on the ground as if being readied for burial. These, we learned, were identical matches to the suspended coffins inside, meaning each county had two copper boxes dedicated to the people lynched there, each person's name inscribed twice.

These outdoor twins were not meant to stay where they were. The Memorial requests that each county come and fetch its box in order to install it at home as its own memorial, an echo of the memorial where we now stood.

The invitation to claim the coffin rendered the memorial a moving one in the literal sense—it was a request requiring action. The day we visited in 2019, though, our students noted, not a single coffin had been claimed.

14.

Action—its efficacy, its volume, and its value—continued to preoccupy me. Then a friend handed me a copy of a small yellow book called *A Field Guide to Climate Anxiety*.

"The myopic focus on action," its author, Sarah Jaquette Ray, writes, "at the expense of theorizing, cultivating collective and personal resilience, and also plain old contemplation is also a kind of anti-intellectualism." I felt called out by this, stung. Ray saw the overemphasis on action that I was all caught up in as part of "a broader cultural shift away from valuing the world of ideas and thinking about the existential questions of life." This shift, she argues, renders such pursuits as privileged folly rather than central activities of being alive and tending to the future. Right action, after all, was the aftermath of contemplation. I mulled over this for days.

Soon it was time to visit the Bureau of Linguistical Reality at the Jewish Museum in San Francisco.

Quante and Escott were seated at a table just inside the museum's entry, sporting matching olive-green jumpsuits adorned with Bureau of Linguistical Reality patches, like subversive femme astronauts, future-bound.

I sat down opposite them, feeling as though I was taking part in something between a Tarot reading and a Catholic confessional, and we began.

"So," I said, "as you know, I'm looking for a word." They nodded. "My word," I fumbled, "well, the word I need is related to a feeling of grief at the state of the planet, but it's about the desire for a memorial, a sort of place to put the grief, or to sit with it, and feel it, or maybe mourn all that's being lost." Quante and Escott nodded again. They could help me, I could sense them saying, but we'd need more specifics.

But see, words were tripping me up again—I still, even after weeks of preparation, couldn't even find the language to describe the word I was lacking.

"Let's back up," Escott suggested. In order to find a word, it would be helpful to home in on a definition. This, though, was part of my problem. I must have seemed hurried, for they took the opportunity to remind me again that creating a new word was a process—one that now included defining my definition—that would take time. This was another dimension of the problem, I noted. It's difficult to access patience in a world in which we're running out of time.

"Yes!" Escott said brightly. This tension between urgency and patience was in part why the Bureau existed in the first place. As Albrecht had posited, the world was changing so rapidly that it left language behind. "The glacial pace of language doesn't work anymore," Escott said. And some of it was simply out of date.

"Think of the adage 'safe as houses,'" Quante offered. What relevance did that saying have now that, between fires and floods and storms, houses weren't equipped to keep us safe?

"So the word you're looking for describes the memorial?" Escott asked. I clarified that it wasn't the memorial itself I wanted a word for, but rather the instinct to make one, or to have one to go to—to just want them to exist.

"I feel like I keep encouraging you to think of memorial as something ephemeral," Quante said, "but you keep coming back to the physical." I acknowledged that she was right, but that thanks in part to her original question, I was no longer tied to the notion of a permanent structure. I'd come across another quote from Maya Lin: "I don't make objects, I make places," places that, she explained, "set a stage for experience and for understanding experience." I thought of the Memorial Riders, Galanin's corn, the mud city that would vanish when the rains eventually came, or, if they never did, would crack and crumble.

"I think I'm looking for something bound by either space or time," I said.

"Hmm," Escott said. "That's interesting."

"Is *bound* the right word here?" Quante wondered. We pondered this for a while. To be bound could speak of constraint, but, I posited, it could also gesture toward interdependence.

"So it's the instinct to make a memorial," Escott said. But even this I had a quibble with. It was not that I myself wanted to make a memorial, but rather that I wanted them to exist.

"Don't worry," Escott said, "we're not giving you the job." Thank goodness, I said, because I couldn't even do this most basic thing: describe the impulse that lacked a word so I could bring a word into being.

Escott asked some additional clarifying questions: Was my desire for memorial a constant feeling—a constant need?

"The instinct to memorialize is relatively constant," I replied, "but the contours of the feeling are different every time."

Escott then wondered if the creation of a single memorial would satisfy my yearning. "Would one be enough?"

This was a great question. And the answer, though I hadn't considered it before, was a resolute *no*. I wanted a multitude of them, perhaps even a movement—or for their cathartic symbolism to be grafted onto the existing climate movement, in all its multitude. I thought about what Doss wrote in *Memorial Mania*, her argument that "contemporary American memorials embody the feelings of particular publics at particular historical moments, and frame cultural narratives about self-identity and national purpose." I wanted the climate movement to be thus embodied, which felt like a precondition of its power. I wanted this clarity of national purpose. I wanted again to mummify the air in the room.

"We're getting somewhere," said Escott.

But how to make a word?

We began speaking of roots, prefixes, and suffixes connoting the various words connected to the word I needed—instinct, memory, grief, mourning, community, ritual, space, place. By now, other visitors had pulled up chairs to join us. Escott turned to the newcomers and gave an overview of my conundrum. What were words we might throw into the collective stew of contemplation? *Cremation* was one that came to mind for her: a word deriving from the Italian *cremare*, to cremate, though -*mation* also gestured at creation, as in *creating* something from the burn. Given the notion of anticipatory grief embedded in my definition, she offered, the prefix *pre-* might do some work, giving us *premation* as a neologism—something that spoke of anticipation, of destruction, of mourning, of making something new.

We spoke and scribbled, winding far away from the original questions, as if we were floating down high water. I was understanding the extent to which their definition-making was a discursive process of probing and association and query. It was frustrating and delightful. Eventually, time-bound as I was, I had to go. We didn't have a full definition yet, or a word, but we were getting somewhere. Or perhaps we were looping in circles. Regardless, the inquiry itself felt like being plugged back into a battery. I was all lit up by words again. They'd be in touch, they told me. I was to expect a Google doc soon.

That night, back at my computer, I considered our draft neologism, *premation*, and spent hours looking up further etymologies and definitions. *Premonition*—knowing something in advance of its happening. I found the word *mariti*—to care for. Wasn't the offering of a memorial space a form of care? *Memorious*: having a good memory. What about the gutting, painful element of this yearning? *Akhos*—a Greek word meaning pain, or ache. *Ache*, that was more right than *yearning*. Why hadn't I thought of that word before?

A few days after our meeting, I got an email from Escott with the promised google doc. She'd assembled a draft definition for my neologism: *premation*.

"A desire to create, hold or cultivate a memorial . . ." it began. "Memorializing a loss that is still ongoing, unfolding. Often this loss is a collective phenomenon, the aftermath of a particular disaster, but also tied to many global disasters linked though the impacts of a worldwide climate crisis. As such the loss often does not have defined scale or borders."

A formal definition of my desire, while still baggy, was finally taking shape. Having it articulated back to me, even in this draft form, gave me great relief. The burden of both definition and longing had become shared.

Even so, I kept on searching for more words, etymological roots and their meanings, as if, rather than merely solving my problem, this neologism exercise had pried open a portal. During the early pandemic, I'd bought a compact edition of the *Oxford English Dictionary*: two giant, blue-spined books nested together inside a box with a drawer that held the magnifying glass required to read the microscopic print. I spread these books out on my kitchen table and removed the magnifying glass, bringing my face close to the page like a detective.

At some point in my associative searching, I arrived at the word *immemorial*. It was almost impossible to read *immemorial* and not think of the phrase *time immemorial*—connoting something ancient, long-lived, some ancestral past. It did have the word memorial in it (though its definition, strictly speaking, had nothing to do with the sort of memorial I was talking about). Because the prefix *im-* can mean both *into* or *toward*, as well as *not*, or something's opposite, the word simultaneously connoted being inside the memorial and being not a memorial at all.

Maybe it needed a suffix, too, something that spoke to the ache and desire to be a part of ancient time, the ache and desire for this memorial space, to be both inside it and to not need it. *Mania* was one—an excessive desire. And then there was *-algia*—another suffix connoting a discomfort disorder, as in *myalgia*, *nostalgia*. It derived from the ancient Greek word that meant both *pain* and *sorrow*. *Immemorialgia*. The sorrowful ache for memorial, to be part of ancient time and to mourn it, to be distinct from memory and deeply nested within it.

These neologisms weren't just about what the parts of the words added up to; they were also the feelings the words connoted, and the associations made through sonic resonance. I was breaking apart language like a giddy scientist and putting it back together again.

15.

During the second pandemic summer, roughly a year before I'd finally become pregnant and during that small slip of time post-vaccine when the world felt like it was opening back up again, jubilant and free and even, perhaps, ripe for true change, I traveled to New York. I was there on another writing assignment and stayed in Manhattan near Madison Square.

One particularly warm night of my stay, my friend Jude walked me back from dinner in the East Village to my hotel. We approached Madison Square Park, closed and empty of people but illuminated in such a way as to highlight, in the center of the fecund, leaf-heavy trees of midsummer, a peculiar thicket of bare white trunks that glowed in the night. There were about forty of these trees, which, upon closer look, were leafless. In fact, they lacked any sign of being alive besides their unmistakable tree form. They were spaced uniformly, and thus somewhat unnaturally, like headstones in a military graveyard. From where we stood, the Empire State Building rose behind them, blazing with artificial life and the relentless commerce of the city. What were these trees, if that's what they were, haunting this small city park on a hot summer evening?

It turned out this was *Ghost Forest*, an installation of some forty Atlantic white cedars—dead

Atlantic white cedars, that is, that had effectively been strangled to death by salinating soils as a result of sea-level rise and storm surges. These trees had once covered more than 500,000 acres on the East Coast of the United States, but today only 10 percent of their habitat remains, leaving them endangered. It also turned out that this installation's architect was Maya Lin.

After Hurricane Sandy, Lin had visited the New Jersey Pine Barrens to behold the wreckage and was rendered speechless by what she saw: large, sweeping forests of leafless tree stalks—miles and miles of tall dead spears, often referred to as *ghost forests*. Where she had once wanted to "cut into the earth" for her Vietnam Veterans Memorial, she was now seeing the earth, in a way, already slashed. "This is the piece," she recalls thinking. "This is what I want to capture." The forest itself was the memorial.

It was just a matter of moving it to a place where it would be more widely seen. She arranged to bring forty-nine of these dead trees from their New Jersey homes to New York City. During winter, she "planted them," when the park's living trees were also leafless in their winter sleep. But as the living trees began to awaken and burst bud in spring, the ghost forest remained dead. The installation would remain in the park for an entire year to complete a full cycle of seasons, the dead trunks contrasting with the movement and change of the still-living trees. But what was remarkable was that even the ghost trees changed with the seasons and over time—"graying out," as Lin put it, as they continued to take on the increasing degradations of death.

Though she started out having made a memorial to the casualties of war, much of Lin's work is now devoted to climate change. "We have very little time," she explained in a recent interview, "but . . . this is a time when you absolutely don't give up, when you work even harder."

Jude and I stood there staring upward. *I make places.* Everything within that muggy night was coated in a sheen of something or other: sprinkler mist upon the grasses, city-slick upon the concrete, sweat upon our brows, and the ghost trees positively glowed, as though bioluminescent, lit from within. Once again, Lin had managed to move me through spatial metaphor.

I wanted to walk beneath these towering corpses. The gate to the park was closed, but Jude and I hopped the fence. The forest was even more beguiling up close. The pallid skin of the trees brought to mind the way my grandmother looked, regal and strange, in her open casket before we closed the lid and buried her.

Like a death mask cast over the face of a dying loved one, *Ghost Forest* was a spectral memorial to the future that commanded visitors' attention and asked us to mourn tomorrow's dead. I imagined these trees drinking in my grief like they once did carbon and light, and metabolizing it into something else—energy, more life. But soon a security guard spotted us and yelled our way, so we ran, jumping back over the fence and hastening back into the ceaseless Manhattan night.

16.

I was certainly drawn to memorials because they worked with material other than words, which bucked my linguistic complacency and, unstuck, helped me feel beneath the stale casings of language. As a journalist, I was particularly moved by Lin's *Ghost Forest* because it was constructed from the very substance of the vanishing, the ultimate primary source. It brought to mind the terrorist bombing memorial in Oslo I'd once visited, built from the blown-out bits of a former building, and an Italian memorial to a farmers' revolt made of the very burlap sacks the farmers used to collect their harvests.

It also brought to mind another installation memorializing the melting glaciers. When a colossal mass calved from the Greenland ice sheet in 2014, artists Olafur Eliasson and Minik Rosing managed to get ahold of some of the rended ice. They hauled twelve separate hunks, each taller than a man, to a central city plaza of Copenhagen, where the Intergovernmental Panel on Climate Change was assembling. Onlookers walked among these melting relics as if visiting Stonehenge or Mayan ruins. Many visitors took photos of the vanishing, not unlike I had done with the dead fish on the beach. Others touched the ice with their bare hands, stood agog, or embraced the ice like one might a dying friend.

★★★

So some of these climate memorials did exist already, I had just had to look. It even turned out that in 2016, long before my own preoccupations with remembering the vanishings had taken me over, the National Parks Service, National Capital Planning Commission, and Van Alen Institute launched a design competition called Memorials for the Future. They solicited proposals, just like the federal government had for the Vietnam Veterans Memorial so many years before, for a memorial to be built in Washington, D.C. The chosen memorial would mark another chapter in the evolving story of memorial design.

"It is not just the past that warrants reflection," the design committee posited; the tools of memorialization could help us grapple with the present too. Entrants were thus asked "to imagine the possible future of memorials: How can they look forward and not only back? How can we commemorate in more adaptive, interactive, and ephemeral ways?"

Though they weren't strictly soliciting climate memorials, the winner of the competition, *Climate Chronograph: A Memorial and Meter for the Future Rising Sea*, would plant a teeming grove of cherry trees at the edge of East Potomac Park—a site that was once, before the Army Corps of Engineers intervened, situated at the bottom of the Potomac River. Here, floods take place with increasing regularity as sea levels begin to rise. The design would grade the grove of cherry trees so that it sloped downward toward the water's edge. Over time, bit by bit, the park would be submerged; benches and walkways and row after row of cherry trees would drown. The memorial was designed to erase itself.

This design derived in part from the ancient Egyptian nilometer, an ancient tool that recorded the Nile's water levels to allow predictions about the future: what the growing season held, whether the people of Egypt could expect droughts or floods. So sacred was this tool that it was often housed deep inside a temple, and only priests and rulers were permitted to read it and cast interpretations of what was in store.

Climate Chronograph would measure things in reverse: it wouldn't offer predictions as to sea-level rise, but instead would mark how much the water had already risen. "One foot of sea-level rise," the proposal explains, "renders four rows of trees dead, bare-branched delineations of shorelines past." The tree death would take place slowly; in the spring, when they burst into pale-pink bloom, the rows of trees would become a gradient of color moving from alive to dead.

"Nature will write our story, our choices, into the landscape," the designers wrote. In this way, writes historian Edward T. Linenthal, "*Climate Chronograph* is a new form of memorialization that commemorates the aftermath of the present."

17.

I had encountered *Climate Chronograph* and Lin's *Ghost Forest* during a tree-book boom—*Finding the Mother Tree*, *The Hidden Life of Trees*, and *The Overstory* were just some of the tree books recently published to much acclaim—when I myself, thick in the zeitgeist, had been writing a lot about trees.

Just before hopping on that plane to New York where I chanced upon *Ghost Forest*, I'd driven to a friend's wedding, which was to be held in a small meadow tucked into the crags of the Eastern Sierra. The route took us through Yosemite, that magnificent granite moonscape, but also through miles upon miles of charred trees. That spring I'd done a lot of driving throughout California, through its cities and backwoods, its deserts and its mountain meadows, its twisting river valleys and agricultural flats. Between

2012 and 2021, one in every eight acres of California burned; in 2021, more than four million acres had been destroyed by fire, and nearly everywhere I went I confronted those excruciating scars.

Part of the trouble with comprehending climate change is that its costs are abstractions until they're at your own door. How about this: the amount of California that had gone missing that year was almost equivalent in size to the state of Massachusetts.

"We're burning here," I'd texted the Massachusetts side of family in September of 2020. For two weeks, those of us in the Bay Area had been living in a hellscape of toxic smoke. We couldn't go outside; we taped up our doorways and windows, bought up all the air purifiers the stores had to offer. Then one day my alarm went off when it was still dark outside. I was sure I'd programmed it wrong. Dazed, I peered at the clock, then out the window, then at the clock again. Seven thirty in the morning, dark as night—as if the sun, so weary with us, had opted not to rise. A thick, impenetrable layer of smoke had accumulated like an umbrella, blocking the light of day. I might have stayed in bed, mourning and cowering, but I had to go to work. I decided to ride my bike instead of drive with the logic that, if my home state was being cremated, I should at least be present for it, prostrate under its remains. I pedaled through that unabating twilight as the particulate wreckage of California blotted the sky. It stayed dark, an eerie orange murk, all day long.

Now, nearly a year later, en route to the wedding, we drove silently through the burn zones, remembering, or struggling to remember, the names and timelines of the fires that had passed through in recent years. We arrived, set up camp, and woke up early with the sun. Because we had some time before the wedding, we decided to visit the mountains on the eastern side of the sweltering Owens Valley, where thousand-year-old groundwater is pumped into aqueducts to keep Los Angeles's pools filled and lawns green. I'd always wanted to visit the Inyo National Forest to see what might just be the world's oldest trees: the bristlecones, some nearly five thousand years old.

It took almost an hour to reach the park from the valley floor, our Prius heaving with effort. The park entrance was situated at about eleven thousand feet above sea level—the air was thin up there, the earth dry. We set off on a four-mile loop from the parking lot on a trail that shot us eastward above another valley facing Nevada. And soon the fabled bristlecones, trunks twisting like gnarled hands, were everywhere.

Trees like redwoods are magnificent for their towering heights; Joshua trees, for their strange, subterranean forms; sequoias, for their remarkable girth. But the bristlecones, old as they were, didn't boast much. They were short, given their age, twenty to thirty feet at most, and appeared more like sculpted artworks than living things: their branches buckled and reached skyward like ragged bones, their bark rough and sturdy like an elephant's hide. Their stooped silhouettes recalled a slowdance in an old folks' home: each step a conjuring of lost time.

Time, for many of us on earth, seems to be speeding up. The habitat the bristlecones are best suited to live in is shifting; the days are becoming hotter, the soil too dry even for these trees built to survive with so little. Not too long from now, all of them will disappear. On our hike, then, we were walking through a miraculous landscape of the past and a ghost forest of the future.

After a few miles we came to what's called the Grove of the Ancients, a cluster of bristlecones that were over four thousand years old. Somewhere in the grove stood Methuselah—the oldest tree in the park, named for the biblical figure who lived for nearly a thousand years. There is no placard or sign announcing Methuselah, though, since the park wants to protect it against poaching or vandalism. I thought of the manatee whose hide was carved up with a human name. We sat in the Grove of the Ancients for a while in silence, listening to our own breath and the nonhuman sounds amid the trees.

By now, everything had started to resemble a memorial. That's the problem with metaphors, symbols. You can really overdo it. At a certain point in my memorial quest, if you caught me in the right mood, you could convince me (or perhaps I'd try to convince you) that my cruddy tube of toothpaste, deformed and half-empty, was a memorial to, I don't know, the perils of waste culture, or lost youth. So yes, I saw the bristlecones, so thick with memory, as physical testimony to the passage of thousands of years of ecological history, as living statuary remembering themselves.

I'd read of a burgeoning movement of ecological personhood: the notion, borrowing from both animistic traditions and the sly tactics of corporate personhood, that trees and rivers and mountains were beings that deserved rights and privileges under the letter of the law. In 2017, for instance, India granted the Ganges and Yamuna Rivers the same legal standing as human beings. In 2018, the city council of Toledo, Ohio, drew up a bill of rights for Lake Erie. In 2022, Panama enacted a law assuring the rights of nature to "exist, persist, and regenerate." Shouldn't the bristlecones enjoy the power of protection?

The trail wound us back to the visitor's center, where I bought a few postcards to send to friends far away. As I went to the register to pay, a ranger walked in the door carrying a stack of plastic flags, soil still clinging to the metal stakes. There were perhaps twenty in her hand, and she waved them toward her coworkers behind the register with a grimace.

"Oh," the woman behind the register said.

"Yes," the ranger replied.

"Oh, no," the woman said again.

"None of them," she said. "None of them made it."

The flags had marked bristlecone seedlings from last spring—hope for the perpetuation of this forest. But all there was to show of them were these uprooted flags of defeat.

The concept of environmental personhood is not without complications. ("Where does a forest begin and end?" asks proponent Robert Macfarlane. "Is a mountain made of the rain it draws down from the clouds as well as the bedrock that gives it altitude?") But I found it magnificent all the same. Like the mother in *The Memory Police* and so many artists I'd been studying, I'd been ordering the world by what was disappearing. This was a way of ordering the world based on intrinsic rights to live.

18.

"I often feel when I am underwater I have entered a dream like state," the British artist Jason DeCaires Taylor has said. "Gravity and reality is suspended. Imagination is endless."

DeCaires Taylor builds museums undersea. He chooses places where the coral reefs have bleached and died away. Scientists predict that by 2050, 90 percent of the world's reefs may be gone. DeCaires Taylor installs sculptures made of nontoxic concrete in these loamy, barren places. In the Yucatán, he cast life-sized forms of people who now stand as "guardians to the sea," as well as a horde of bankers stooped in prayer as a commentary to the role the financial systems play in environmental collapse. ("Each Banker has a cavity between his buttocks for marine life to inhabit. Crustaceans and eels make this space their home," he writes.) In Lanzarotte, a Spanish colony in the Canary Islands, he built "The Raft of Lampedusa," depicting thirteen refugees traveling, Europe-bound, on a precarious inflatable raft.

Over time, what begin as white-gray statues built in his London studio soon begin to shape-shift. The sea itself takes over, marine life begins to colonize the forms cast in stone. First come the algae or sea slime; later, if things go as planned, they become home again to coral reefs. Though part of the beauty of the work, as de Caires Taylor explained it to me, is that there's no reliable plan. The sea life will do what it will; each time he visits his underwater museums he encounters entirely new worlds. The oldest among them resemble ruins, the original forms sometimes barely recognizable.

DeCaires Taylor builds his museums in underwater locations people can visit with snorkels or scuba gear or glass-bottomed boat. The idea is to bring more people into direct, awestruck encounter with the sea. The sea itself, he said, is "the most beautiful museum in the world."

One of the reasons people enjoy art, writes Rachel Cusk in *The Last Supper*, is that "each object represents another triumph for love, for survival, for care. Each object can be placed on the scales against man's violence and destructiveness. Which way the scale will tip at the end of it all, no one knows." These words echo the placard's inscription atop the now-dead glacier—*only you will know if we succeeded.*

A few years ago, off the southern coast of Cyprus, DeCaires Taylor built an enchanted forest where human figures walk, stare, and dream. One recurring figure is a small child who holds up a camera to the rest, as if to capture the world that remains, and also as if to say: I'm watching.

★★★

There was a baby on the way, and I still had a catalog of worries about what life, the Earth, had in store; all the birdsong she'd never hear, the fish she'd never see, the trees that would burn or desiccate long before she ever greeted them. Ben wrote a poem that spring called "Waiting for My Daughter to Be Born." *I lie down to sleep and / love swirls inside / my skull like 10,000 silver mackerel. / Up from the depths, the sea lions come, / baring their teeth, barking / all the ways the world will harm her.*

How would we decide what to tell her of the world versus what to leave for her to narrate in a language of her own?

I came back to this Magnason quote again and again: "When a system collapses, language is released from its moorings. Words meant to encapsulate reality hang empty in the air, no longer applicable to anything. . . . People suddenly find it difficult to hit upon the right phrasing, to articulate concepts that match their reality."

Slowly, slowly, Ben's poem continues, *the shark comes, / wearing the plundered face / of the future.*

Because time plods forward, the future arrived. I gave birth to the baby. It took four days of labor to bring her into the world. During the last two minutes, before they sliced me open, it seemed clear that she would die. I spent many months stuck in the memory of those final minutes, as if in a loop. Though she was right there in her bassinet breathing, there was a part of me that didn't believe either of us had made it to the other side. It wasn't until I began to write about that time, to put it into words, that my grief took shape and the memory, slowly, found release. I wasn't a builder. The tools I had to nurse my memory and my grief, however incomplete, were words.

In time, the baby began to reach out her hands to touch things. She began to roll from side to side, and then onto her stomach. She began to crawl, to lift herself onto her feet, to walk and then to run. This was all lovely to watch, but only because she was mine. On a basic level I knew it wasn't all that remarkable, just the standard stuff of living. Then she began to say words. First came the nouns (*shoe*, *bird*, *cat*, *bath*, *tree*) and then the desires (*more*, *no*), and then came the feelings (*hungry*, *tired*, *scared*, *safe*). This was the opposite of semantic satiation—with her, words were new again.

But most remarkable was when she began to communicate her memory. At just a year and a half, she wanted to talk, in her slapdash language, about what had happened during her day: the turkeys we'd met at the park, the blood blister I'd given her when accidentally clipping a tag of skin between the buckles of her bike helmet. We reenacted this offense again and again, her pointing to her bike helmet and then to me. "Ouchie!" she'd say. "Helmet, Mama, ouch!" I'd apologize, assuring her I'd be more careful this time, that, in at least this one tiny dimension within my control, the future held better things for her. Another time, a metal shelf fell next to her in the bathtub. For months, her favorite game was to take my hand and drag me into the bathroom, pointing to the shelf with a long face and looking at me expectantly until I said, "I'll protect you!" in a singsong voice and drew her close. She loved this ritual of call and response to her fears.

"You're choosing the future," Rebecca Solnit said to me when first I told her I was pregnant. And now here this baby was, a person cataloging the flowers we walked by on the street. She would miss them when they disappeared. Like the mother in *The Memory Police*, I felt compelled to be some kind of memory keeper. But I was also a memory maker, facilitating my child's encounters with the world. Just before my daughter turned two, CAConrad came out with a new book of poems called *Listen to the Golden Boomerang Return*. This one was full of ritual poetry not for the extinct, but for those creatures who had managed to survive, written because the poet longed "to / desire / the world / as it is / not as / it was."

On the fjordal coast of Norway, DeCaires Taylor created an underwater sculpture near a children's museum. On a stone dock stand a father and daughter made of stone. Hand in hand, they look down into the deep where ten more human figures are tethered to the seafloor by what resembles an umbilical cord.

This sculpture is a gift for the future, *our invitation*, as Rozic said of his camera obscura, *from darkness*. For over time, the statue will become a living thing. My daughter is alive in a time of vanishings, but she, too, is a creature of memory. Let our grief become fuel. Let us desire the world as it is. Look, you can already see it, all that algae, those coral polyps, the mussels and crabs. The wordless stone is turning to life.

ACKNOWLEDGMENTS

Thank you to the many writers, thinkers, and artists whose work guided my thinking, and complicated it, during the writing of *Immemorial*. I cite many works, artists, and texts directly in these pages, though many others influenced me greatly in the wings. Thank you especially to the Bureau of Linguistical Reality, Nicholas Galanin, Janko Rosic and the members of Sestava, Peter Romavh, Rebecca Solnit, and Jason DeCaires Taylor for taking the time to speak with me about their art and ideas. Thank you, too, to the many people fighting for climate justice and those holding the flame of futurist imagination.

Much gratitude to the teachers, writers and editors who have supported my work related to the environment and climate change over the years. Some of the material in this book originally appeared in two essays published on Literary Hub: "A Totalitarian Inheritance" and "The Land of Smoke and Fire."

The Silvers Grant for Work in Progress supported the research for this book, and thus made it possible to write it.

All hail independent presses. Thank you to the excellent people at Transit Books for patiently shepherding this book into being and for taking such good care of its becoming. It's an honor and delight to be published by you.

My father passed away as I was finishing this book. His death taught me about the cavernous dimensions of grief, but first, in life, he taught me how to love the world and its imperfections. I'm so grateful to him.

Thanks to Ben for his belief in my work, his devotion to the planet, and his perpetual encouragement toward slowness and attention. And thank you, Clio, to whom this book is dedicated, for the gift of determined, exuberant life. Yes, indeed, we chose the future.

LAUREN MARKHAM is the author of the award-winning *The Far Away Brothers: Two Young Migrants and the Making of an American Life* and *A Map of Future Ruins*. Her work has appeared in *VQR*, *Harper's*, *The New York Times Magazine*, *The Guardian*, *The New York Review of Books*, and other publications.

Undelivered Lectures is a narrative nonfiction series featuring book-length essays in slim, handsome editions.

Transit Books is a nonprofit publisher of international and American literature, based in Berkeley, California. Founded in 2015, Transit Books is committed to the discovery and promotion of enduring works that carry readers across borders and communities. Visit us online to learn more about our forthcoming titles, events, and opportunities to support our mission.

TRANSITBOOKS.ORG